Contents

A Practical Approach to Financial Management

Third Edition

R. Dixon

First published in Great Britain 1978 by Financial Training Publications Limited, Avenue House, 131 Holland Park Avenue, London W11 4UT

ISBN: 1 85185 029 5

Typeset by LKM Typesetting Ltd, London EC1
Printed by Redwood Burn, Trowbridge

To Dorothy and Joyce

Introduction

The task of financial management is to facilitate the achievement of organisation objectives by obtaining financial resources and then using them profitably and effectively.

A financial resource may be cash, but equally it may be a bank overdraft or creditors, who are in fact unpaid suppliers and who in effect supply short-term credit. Whatever the source of the finance the end result is that the finance enables an organisation to spend money.

Two of the major functions of any manager are planning and control. Planning may be defined as forecasting the likely outcome of a particular course of action in terms of it bringing the achievement of objectives or goal. If a particular course of action is forecast as a means of successfully achieving objectives it will be adopted as the plan. The control function then involves monitoring the implementation of the plan to check for any deviation, and then modifying the plan if necessary. The two functions are closely linked — without control, planning is ineffective.

As far as the financial manager is concerned, the planning and control functions are evident in the following ways. First, he needs to plan the financial strategy of the business; this involves setting the financial objectives of the organisation and deciding the amount of money which should be spent, on what it should be spent, etc. The financial manager also needs to plan and control the financing of working capital both by means of self-financing through trade credit, and also from other sources of finance, ensuring that these other sources are obtained when necessary. Finally, the financial manager needs to plan and control the use of funds for long-term investment; this may involve using fixed assets or the purchase of investments in other businesses.

1 Company finance and financial management

FINANCIAL MANAGEMENT

Financial management can be defined as 'the management process of planning the provision, generation and conservation of financial resources'.

The financial manager must perform a number of functions as part of the general management function. Two of the major functions of management are planning and controlling.

The planning function involves a number of steps:

(a) identifying opportunities;
(b) determining/defining goals and objectives;
(c) evaluating alternatives that might lead towards the goals;
(d) policy formulation plan;
(e) quantification and communication;
(f) implementation;
(g) review.

In the most general terms planning is, in effect, deciding what to do and how to do it.

The control function then involves a monitoring of actual events against the plan, and the taking of prompt action where there is deviation from the plan, to ensure that actual results conform as nearly as possible to the plan.

Financial management has both theoretical and practical dimensions. The theory is based on models which are quite artificial but knowledge of which is needed by the financial manager in his practical function. Finally, we may note that while much of financial management is essentially *internal* to the firm, it is all ultimately reflected *externally* in the form of the firm's external financial reports.

BUSINESS OBJECTIVES

The objectives of a firm are often many and varied, including public and social responsibility, profitability, productivity, market standing, and development.

Although those involved in business seek to increase their wealth it is not possible for this in itself to be the sole objective, because a firm can only make/ increase wealth by attracting customers to the product or service it is supplying. Thus the main objectives of any business undertaking must be twofold:

(a) *Marketing objectives*   It must offer something which is special, unique, or plainly what people want.

(b) *Financial objectives*   It must be noted that marketing and financial objectives go hand in hand: marketing objectives are pointless unless they increase wealth and also they cannot be achieved without financial support, whilst financial objectives will not be achieved without adequate marketing objectives.

The financial objectives of a business are twofold, i.e., 'making a profit' and 'staying in existence'.

MAKING A PROFIT

Profit can be defined as 'the difference between the amount of cash invested and the amount of cash returns in the form of distributions during the life of the business or in the form of a terminal distribution when all assets have been realised and creditors paid'. Whilst a company is still in business there is no profit other than cash and no profit other than the difference between cash introduced by the proprietors or shareholders and the cash they eventually withdraw.

Example   Mr Justinuff buys some sports clothing and equipment for £1,000 and runs a retail business for three years. His reported profits are as follows:

Year	Sales	Purchases and expenses	Depreciation	Net profit (loss)
	£	£	£	£
1	500	360	333	(193)
2	1,200	690	333	177
3	1,500	900	334	266
	3,200	1,950	1,000	250

The cash flows were as follows — assuming debtors take three months to pay and Mr Justinuff pays his expenses on average two months late.

Year	Cash received from debtors £	Cash paid to creditors £	Net cash flow £
1	3/4 × 500 = 375	5/6 × 360 = 300	75
2	From yr 1:125	From yr 1:60	390
	3/4 × 1,200 = 900	5/6 × 690 = 575	
3	From yr 2:300	From yr 2:115	560
	3/4 × 1,500 = 1,125	5/6 × 900 = 750	
4	From yr 3:375	From yr 3:150	225

	1,250
Less: initial layout	1,000
Therefore cash gain =	250

It is evident that incremental cash received over the life of the business is (and must be) the same as total profit, although year by year the cash flow is likely to be completely different from the reported profit figures.

OBJECTIVES AFFECTING PROFIT TARGETS

It is evident that a profit needs to be made by a business in order to provide a desirable increment of cash. The amount of profit, however, depends on the purpose to which it is to be put.

Stability

Profits are needed in order to replace fixed assets as they become worn out, and unfixed (current) assets as they are sold and used. Most accounting systems seek to determine profit after making charges against revenue to provide for the maintenance of capital. This is possible where prices are stable, but historical cost accounts are unable to do this where price increases are significant. For the stability of the business to be ensured in this situation, the profit must be enough to cover any enhanced costs of asset maintenance.

The need for profit to ensure stability is evident in another sense. An organisation subject to fluctuations in activity will be subject to high profits in peak periods but must endure low takings in trough periods. The profits of peak periods will help to ensure survival in trough periods. In this sense stability is closely allied to liquidity.

Business growth

The objective of 'business growth' is a factor which determines the amount of profit needed. Before we examine the relationship between business growth and profit, however, we must define and gain a correct understanding of what business growth is. The following example may provide this understanding. A company may invest £500,000 extra in fixed assets without increasing the number of items or the output capacity; this is not growth, it is merely increasing the worth of the assets, or reflecting an increase in prices. Real growth only exists after the net operating assets of the business have been preserved. Yet it must be noted that growth in assets is also only relevant to business objectives if the extra or more expensive capital equipment will enable increased profits to be made.

Similarly, growth in sales is only relevant if it contributes to the improvement of total profit. In both areas justification for growth can also be based on the part it plays in preventing the loss of business to a competitor.

The amount of profit needed for the purpose of business growth is determined by a number of factors. It is evident that profits alone cannot finance growth; outside resources will be needed, i.e., long-term capital in the form of loans, shares, etc. The retention of profits to finance 'normal growth' (i.e., excluding the development of new product, takeovers, technological changes), is a policy pursued by some companies. Such a policy, however, is dependent on the normal amount of profit and the normal rate of growth for that particular business. Its desirability depends upon the company's dividend policy.

Returns to investors and participators

If we look at the basic requirements of an organisation we will be able to identify progressively the investors and participators, the returns they seek to gain and how this affects the amount of profit the organisation needs to make. We can identify three essential ingredients needed by a company for survival: ideas for products and their market; skills to carry out the necessary activities; and money.

Ideas will be obtained by the organisation from people they employ or from outside; in the latter case these ideas must be purchased. A clear example of purchasing an idea from outside the organisation is evident when an inventor registers his innovation with the Patent Office and then allows other people to use it on payment of a fee. The organisation may pay the inventor either by means of a lump sum or by periodic payments. There is a greater risk for the inventor in accepting the latter form of payment because it depends upon the success of his invention. To ease this risk he may also ask for a share in the profits, which, as he is a supplier to the business and not a participator, will never be less than zero.

Secondly, an organisation needs skills; these are purchased by wages and salaries. Wages can be regarded as monetary return or reward for the skills of the employees, and profits are needed to provide this reward. This reward is negotiated at a fixed rate and whilst the business is still in operation it does not fall below a fixed minimum. The 'wage reward' may also be partly made up by an element of profit sharing. The employees are participators in the business and the risk they take is that the firm may at some point in its existence no longer require their skills.

The final essential ingredient, upon which an organisation's survival depends, is money. An organisation may acquire money in the form of loan capital. This is borrowed money, borrowed on terms by which the lender is entitled to a fixed rate of interest and to repayment of his loan at a fixed time. The loan may be secured or unsecured; in the former case security is provided by an asset or group of assets; in the latter there is no security provided and therefore the lender often seeks a high rate of interest to cover his risk. Although those who lend capital on this basis take a risk, the risk only lasts for the duration of the loan and is therefore short-term in comparison with that of the employee whose commitment is potentially lifelong.

Loan capital is not the only source of money available to an organisation, and there are a number of reasons why money is needed from a source other than loan capital. First, long-term capital is needed for long-term fixed assets; this may be obtained in the form of a capital fund which needs no repayment as long as the company exists. Second, there is also need for capital which will only be repaid when a profit exists to pay it. Loan capital is repayable irrespective of profit or loss and is not particularly suitable if profits are unstable. Third, capital is also needed where suppliers would be willing to defer any claims should the business be discontinued, thus giving trade creditors a better chance of distribution.

In effect, the above describes a creditor or supplier of capital who cannot expect remuneration until the company is wound up and all other liabilities paid, and who will receive intermediate payments only when profits are made. Such suppliers are shareholders, who run the risk of complete loss and are therefore entitled to all profits. They own the company and have the right to appoint its board of directors.

The amount of profit needed to remunerate shareholders may be regarded as 'as much as possible', i.e., the management should aim to maximise wealth accruing to ordinary shareholders, subject to the constraints of other interests.

Maximisation of shareholder wealth is more than profit maximisation; it means using profits as dividend distributions and retentions in the business in such a way that between buying his shares and selling them the shareholder maximises his profit.

In order to maximise shareholder wealth the organisation must face two difficulties. The first of these is estimating the shareholders' preference for dividends now or capital gains later. The second is knowing what capital gain the shareholder will obtain; this is difficult because shares are most often bought through an intermediary — the Stock Exchange — and are subject to influences beyond the company's control. Although we cannot discuss fully these problems in this chapter we can note two alternative views with regard to shareholders' rights which may throw further light on the subject.

First, the board of directors frequently does not seek to maximise shareholder wealth, for although in theory shareholders control the board, few bother to exercise control. Consequently the board can use residual profits for long-term development. Second, if the shareholders do not take up the residual profits then other parties are entitled to them i.e., employees. These parties with an interest in the business influence business objectives and goals according to their relative bargaining powers, social attitudes within a community and the political system of the country, etc.

FIXING PROFIT TARGETS

There are a number of rules which govern the task of profit planning and control. One such rule is based on the assumption that profits are primarily earned for shareholders, although it must be noted that profit maximisation for shareholders needs to be worked out in relation to the amount of capital that has been used to achieve the profit if it is to be a sound objective. In reality the objective should be to maximise profit per unit of shareholders' capital invested. This may be either profit per share or profit per £1 book value of capital employed. Calculation of profit per share is a sound approach but it has a major weakness in that it is no use for comparison with other companies because share values vary between companies.

The most consistently reliable measure of the intrinsic value of shares is the value of the net assets they represent expressed in terms of the balance sheet figure of shareholders' capital employed. Thus profitability can be expressed as the maximisation of:

$$\frac{\text{Profit attributable to ordinary shareholders}}{\text{Balance sheet value of shareholders' capital employed}}$$

A weighted average rate of return required on total capital employed will be calculated — the achievement of which will be the responsibility of the managing director. Thus the internal objective will be expressed as:

$$\frac{\text{Profit before loan interest and capital}}{\text{Total capital employed}}$$

Funds which are invested outside the business or are used to meet dividend and interest payments can be segregated leaving the formula for the rate of return on operating assets as follows:

$$\frac{\text{Operating profit before tax}}{\text{Operating capital employed}}$$

STAYING IN EXISTENCE

Earlier we noted that as well as making a profit the financial objective of an organisation was to stay in existence. In the long term this requires the ability to replace assets by generating sufficient profits. In the short term a firm must be able to meet its immediate liabilities. The 'liquidity' of the company is a measure of its ability to meet immediate liabilities, and control of liquidity requires planning and control of cash flows.

ACHIEVING OBJECTIVES: THE DEVELOPMENT OF STRATEGIES

Once objectives have been defined management needs to decide how to achieve them. The business of how to achieve objectives is expressed or formulated in a hierarchy of plans. First come strategic plans, involving broad decisions about matters such as what product, what technology, which markets and involving an evaluation of the alternative strategies by which the firm might achieve its goals. Detailed investment decisions need to be made within these strategies. These relate to decisions regarding expenditure on marketing campaigns, financial support for research — decisions which require thorough financial appraisal. A second level of planning is short term. This involves developing short-term plans which are compatible with strategic objectives and developing divisional and departmental plans of action and targets for subsequent performance measurement.

FINANCIAL CONTROL

Control is a major function of management. Financial control requires feedback of data and follow-up of variance from plans in terms of analyses of causes and responsibilities and action to re-align future performance.

SUMMARY

Planning and control are the major functions of management, with the former involving setting objectives and formulating strategies. The objectives are split into the marketing objectives and the financial objectives. There are two aspects to the financial objectives — making a profit and staying in business. There are three basic purposes for making a profit: stability, growth, and provision of rewards. The amount of profit to be made depends on the purpose.

The shareholders are the principal risk-takers and therefore the major purpose of making profits is to maximise shareholder wealth, or, more specifically, to maximise the rate of return on shareholder's capital.

2 Government action and financial management

THE ECONOMIC BACKGROUND

Businessmen, politicians, the public, foreign traders, etc., are all factors which influence the economy, the availability and cost of funds, and the possibilities of investment within the economy.

The costs incurred in putting supplies on the market take a number of forms: wages, profits, rent and interest. These payments act as income for the recipients and consequently provide a measure of the money value of potential demand for goods and services available.

Demand for goods can be reduced by reducing immediate purchasing power. This can be done by taxation, which redistributes purchasing power through the medium of social services and other government expenditure. It can also be done by saving; this feeds purchasing power back into the system through private and corporate investment. Both these actions in effect delay the emergence of demand.

Where demand exceeds supply there is an inflationary gap — bridged by increases in the selling price. It is against this background that we review government action which can assist or impede the task of financial management.

GOVERNMENT FINANCIAL POLICY

In general terms the impact of government action will be felt in six main ways:

(a) credit restriction;
(b) taxation;
(c) control of wages, dividends and profit;
(d) control of imports and exports;
(e) encouragement of productive investment;
(f) encouragement of personal savings.

Credit restriction

Credit may be restricted in a number of ways:

  (a) legislation for high initial payments;
  (b) through the banking system;
  (c) through the government's national debt operations.

The ability of the banks to provide commercial credit can be reduced by the government funding part of its short-term borrowings from this source, which would tie up a greater proportion of the bank's resources. The Bank of England, acting on the government's behalf, can also call in 'special deposits', which would immobilise part of the banks' resources and also reduce their lending base. Also the amount of money available in bank deposits will be affected by the offering or redemption of government bonds. Such transactions will have a direct influence on interest rates.

The restriction of credit and an increase in interest rates will have a number of effects. It will make borrowing more difficult and less attractive and cause a drop in the value of ordinary shares. It will also increase the cost of capital for the purposes of investment evaluation. Finally, it will reduce demand and thus discourage increases in productive capacity.

Taxation

Taxation can reduce the amount of money in circulation, to the extent that it does not re-emerge through social service and other government expenditure. Incomes generated by the various factors of production can also be redistributed by taxation. The acceptability of investment projects can be very much affected by corporation tax, and the relief given for investment is fixed.

Control of wages, dividends and profit

The object of wages and dividends control is to limit demand for consumer goods within available supplies and hopefully release supplies for export trade.

Profit control is in conflict with this in that it tends to restore home demand and discourage productive investment.

Control of imports and exports

Import control may be facilitated by customs duties and other fiscal devices, whilst exports can be encouraged either by tax allowances or by relief from price and profit controls. When a country is heavily dependent on overseas trade the operation of such controls may be favourable to the exchange rate of its currency but may at the same time damage the internal balance of the economy and discourage productive enterprise.

Encouragement of productive investment

The main forms of encouragement are taxation adjustments, grants or loans for investment in selected areas, and other 'depressed area' incentives such as contributions towards wages.

Encouragement of personal savings

Two examples of encouragement of personal savings include issue of government bonds and tax concessions.

As well as providing a means of personal saving the issue of government bonds provides finance for government borrowing requirements — such bonds provide 71% of the total money raised by government between 1977 and 1982. The effect of this on the stock market is evident. The insurance companies and pension funds have shifted a large share of their money into government hands, quite voluntarily. The life insurance companies, for example, invested some 30% of their new funds in government securities in the period 1970 to 1975; between 1977 and 1981, the proportion rose to over 50%. Pension funds, which invest a lower proportion of their funds in gilt-edged because of the nature of their future obligations, raised their share from 20% in 1970-75 to 30% by the start of the 1980s. This represented an annual investment in government stocks by both types of funds of some £4.2 billion in 1981 alone.

Tax concessions can affect the types of savings and investment, which in turn can bring distortions in the capital market. In recent years it has been evident that the types and percentages of new capital raised by companies have been greatly influenced by tax concessions. The rules by which company taxation is calculated afford certain reliefs which effectively reduce the cost of company distributions to users of funds. Tax relief has been greater for loan finance than for preference share finance, and hence companies wishing to raise fixed-interest capital have for many years been more attracted to new loan/debt finance than to preference share issues.

The taxation benefits which tend to reduce the cost of loan interest below that of a preference dividend of the same percentage rate, also apply to a net-of-tax comparison between the cost of loan interest and ordinary share dividends. A tax benefit in favour of loan interest has always existed but various changes in tax rules have recently reduced the advantage enjoyed by loan finance.

THE SCOPE OF GOVERNMENT ACTION

The scope of government action designed to help business enterprise includes the following.

Enterprise zones

The government has created a number of enterprise zones in areas of England, Scotland, Wales and Northern Ireland with problems of economic and physical decay.

The purpose of these zones is to test, as an experiment, how far industrial and commercial activity can be encouraged by the removal of, or streamlined administration of, certain statutory or administrative controls.

Enterprise zones are designated to run for a period of 10 years subject to renewal, and both new and existing businesses in the zones will be able to benefit from the following measures:

(a) 100% capital allowances for commercial and industrial buildings;
(b) exemption from general rates on industrial and commercial property;
(c) simplification of planning procedures;
(d) exemption from the scope of industrial training boards, not only from the training levy but also from the provision of information.

Business Expansion Scheme

Small firms can raise capital by attracting outside independent investors to subscribe for new, full-risk equity in business. To encourage this the Business Expansion Scheme offers such investors tax incentives when they invest in new ordinary shares issued by certain firms qualifying under the scheme.

Loan Guarantee Scheme

Support is available to help potentially viable small businesses, particularly those unable to provide security to raise medium-term loans from banks and other financial institutions where these are not available on normal commercial terms.

The support is selective and offered only in suitable cases. Sole traders, partnerships, cooperatives or limited companies are eligible for guarantees. Applications will not be considered from large businesses. In determining size, firms with broadly similar ownership or control will be considered as one unit. Applications will not be considered where the owner or controlling group have previously made a claim under the guarantee arrangements. Also a number of specified activities are not eligible, including: agriculture and horticulture, banking and finance, education, house and estate agencies, postal and telecommunication services, medical and health services, night-clubs and licensed clubs, railways, travel agencies, tied public houses.

The support takes the form of a loan guarantee by the Department of Trade and Industry covering repayment of 70% of medium-term loans to eligible small businesses. In consideration for the guarantee the DTI will charge a quarterly premium — this runs at a rate of 5% of the guaranteed amount of the total loan adding 3.5% per annum to the costs of borrowing. The premium will reduce as the loan is repaid. Guarantees cover one or a number of loans up to £75,000 maximum, and will be repayable over periods of between two and seven years.

No personal assets or personal guarantees will be taken as security to cover any part of a guaranteed loan. Before a DTI guarantee can be considered, business owners must have already fully committed any personal assets to secure conventional term loans. The owner(s) must also be prepared to pledge all available business assets as security for guaranteed loans. Before accepting an application the banks and financial institutions involved will need to measure the commitment of the applicants to the success of their business.

Finally, the applicants for the guarantee scheme will be expected to provide information on management, product, market, business history, objectives, financial projections, finance required, security available, principal risks and the management information systems used by the business. During the operation of the scheme additional information of a financial nature must be given to the DTI, i.e., comparison of cash flow and profit and loss figures deviating from earlier plans.

Regional selective assistance

Grants are made available on a selective basis for manufacturing and service projects in the 'assisted areas' which create or safeguard employment. The amount of the support grant is usually negotiated and will be at least the minimum necessary to ensure the project goes ahead.

There are two main forms of selective support: project grants, which are based on the capital costs of a project and on the number of jobs to be created or maintained; and training grants, which are based on training costs associated with manufacturing and service projects. Project grants are related either to fixed capital costs or the number of jobs to be created within three years of the project's start. Training grants relate to training directly associated with a manufacturing or service project and which is essential to the success of the project.

For support to be considered eligible, projects must:

(a) either create new employment or safeguard existing employment in the assisted area;

(b) bring an identifiable regional and national benefit.

The project must be commercially viable.

Regional development grants

The arrangements for regional development grants were revised in November 1984. Under the new arrangements RDGs are available towards the assets and jobs provided as part of approved projects in development areas.

The grant for a project is calculated as the higher of either:

(a) 15% of eligible capital expenditure; or

(b) £3,000 for each new job created.

The amount of grant payable may be subject to the following limits:

(a) Grants per job limit: where projects are carried out by firms employing more than 200 full-time employees, any capital grant payable will be limited to £10,000 for each additional new job created.

(b) The grant per job limit does not affect projects by firms employing less than 200 employees where capital expenditure on the project is less than £500,000. Where capital expenditure by such firms is greater than £500,000, the grant is limited to £75,000 unless a larger sum can be paid under the terms above.

(c) European net grants equivalent limit: for manufacturing projects and service projects undertaken by manufacturers, any job grant payable will be limited to 40% of initial capital investment.

CONCLUSION

The financial manager must face a number of pressures and controls which may appear to be acting contrary to the good of his organisation. The manager must be ready to respond to an ever-changing environment and circumstances. The combination of national controls and individual enterprise creates a 'mixed economy', the justification for which is that in the long run it will yield an economic balance of greatest benefit to the community.

3 Ratio analysis

THE NATURE AND PURPOSE OF RATIO ANALYSIS

The management of a company's finances draws heavily upon the tool of ratio analysis, which is fundamental to the interpretation of accounting data. The calculation of a ratio in any sphere of activity involves the manipulation of two numbers. The accuracy of the result as an indicator of performance, etc., is dependent upon the accuracy with which the original numbers reflect the actual values involved. Accounting data are crucially influenced by the accounting procedure adopted. An additional problem is the rapidity with which data becomes obsolete; obtaining information from balance sheets which reflect performance some time in the past could, instead of being helpful, be misleading.

The problems inherent in ratio analysis will become more apparent as each ratio is considered. The pitfalls examined bring the process into question. Ratio analysis finds its defence in the argument that two numbers are more helpful than one, as shown by the following figures. A profit of £100,000 may seem acceptable, but in what context? A profit figure of this order on a turnover of £800,000 is clearly an improvement on the same profit for a turnover of £100 million. A raw figure can thus be placed in an appropriate context by using a ratio. However, the key to effective ratio analysis is realising that an organisation is not simply two-dimensional and consequently a ratio formed from two sets of data must be examined in the light of a company's operations and situation.

Ratios are used by different groups for different purposes. Management will often use them for purposes of internal control and comparison with competitors' performances. This is not the only way in which ratios impinge upon the company's operations. Potential creditors will frequently use ratios in order to establish the reliability of the organisation in meeting its debts. Investors will utilise any possible source of information to establish the value of an investment in the equity of a company. The final section of this chapter considers the empirical evidence of ratio analysis for predicting success or failure.

The essence of ratio analysis is to quantify key relationships between variables in operating statements, balance sheets, etc., and thus assist in the evaluation of managerial and operational performance. The type of analysis and the importance of the category of ratio will depend upon the interest of the party undertaking the study. The organisation itself will use ratios for the purpose of internal control and to ensure conditions required by suppliers of finance are met.

Financial analysis involves two broad comparisons. The first is historical in nature, contrasting the company's present and perhaps expected future performance with indicators of past achievements. Any trends established may help the analyst to evaluate managerial performance in the light of knowledge relating to general economic changes. Secondly, interfirm comparison (or comparison with industry averages) indicates the relative strength of any one company. Raw data could be misleading unless comparison is made, considering not only industry averages but also dispersion around the norm. There are organisations which provide the necessary databank broken down into appropriate statistics to facilitate comparison.

The two broad categories of comparison, historical and interfirm, both require some form of standardisation of data to allow sensible comparison. Consequently, sound judgement requires strenuous effort to compare like with like. Appropriate data should be for the same point in time, preferably using similar accounting practices, or adjustments will be necessary to take variations into account.

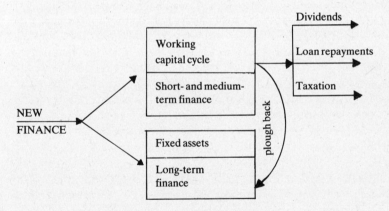

Figure 1   The enterprise as a financial model

Figure 1 illustrates how important it is for any organisation to control costs within the working capital cycle, to establish efficiency criteria for the flow of funds between short-term and long-term assets and liabilities, and also to achieve a satisfactory profit. Each of these three groups of ratios will be considered.

PROFITABILITY

Potential and existing shareholders in an organisation will seek a satisfactory
return from their investment. Dominating much of their considerations will be
measures of the company's profitability in order to establish if they are likely to
obtain wealth through either growth in dividends or capital values. It is for this
reason that much of the layman's use of ratio analysis has been in this area. To a
certain extent these ratios can be seen as spin-off from the control of the flow of
funds and costs.

Two main types of ratio relating to profit exist: profit with respect to sales,
and profit with respect to investment. A closer examination of these two ratios
inevitably indicates a close relationship, demonstrated in the following
equation:

$$\frac{\text{Profit}}{\text{Sales}} \times \frac{\text{Sales}}{\text{Capital}} = \frac{\text{Profit}}{\text{Capital}}$$
$$\text{(A)} \qquad\qquad \text{(B)} \qquad\qquad \text{(C)}$$

Expressing this more fully, the equation shows that the speed with which assets
are utilised (B) multiplied by the profit margin (A) indicates the return on
capital employed (C). This illustrates the interdependence of many groups of
ratios. The analysis can be subdivided into component ratios for (A), (B) and
(C), as shown in Table 1.

Table 1   Profitability ratios

(A) Profit margin*	(B) Speed or Intensity†	(C) Return on capital invested*
Gross profit/Sales	Sales/Fixed assets	Profits/Net assets
Net profit/Sales	Sales/Working capital	Profits/Gross assets
		Profits/Equity capital

* Expressed as a percentage.
† Expressed as number of times per annum.

Changing the emphasis in column (B) from the numerator to the denominator
gives greater emphasis to the control of costs; these ratios are covered in the
next section.

Gross profit margin

This ratio may be defined as:

$$\frac{\text{Sales} - \text{Cost of goods sold}}{\text{Sales}}$$

It indicates something about the efficiency of a company's operations, and is also a reflection of pricing policy.

Net profit margin

This ratio is:

$$\frac{\text{Net profit before tax}}{\text{Sales}}$$

It uses sales as the yardstick to assess a company's ability through time to contain costs or to increase selling price or sales volume. When considered in relation to the ratio for gross profit the two ratios can provide considerable insight. Parallel movements, through time, may indicate stable efficiency; however, divergence between the two ratios can provide a useful warning light that returns are either falling or rising because of a change in the costs of the organisation. Both ratios are pre-tax although it can be argued that managerial efficiency involves tax planning.

Profit margins in isolation can be misleading because of the nature of the goods that different companies produce and sell. In some industries the speed of asset utilisation is very low but the profit margin may be high to compensate for this factor. Producers of power turbines, for example, are unlikely to have rapid utilisation of working capital. Column (C) in Table 1 sets out the ratios relevant to the return on capital employed, which are in many situations more germane to the requirements of shareholders, as they give some indication of the efficiency of the organisation and the likely distribution of any profits achieved between equity payment and the claims of debt finance. The main ratio in this category is return on capital employed.

Return on capital employed (ROCE)

This ratio, sometimes referred to as the 'primary ratio', is:

$$\frac{\text{Operating profit for the period}}{\text{Average capital employed}}$$

It measures the profit generated by each £1 of capital employed as an indication of the productivity of capital. The denominator refers to an average calculated on a time-weighted basis to allow for any new capital infusion during the period.

Inflation has had a major impact on ROCE as a yardstick of performance. The early 1970s gave rise to several companies who had high returns on capital whilst facing very serious cash crises. Whereas current cost accounting provides adjustments that help to put the evaluation of ROCE in a better perspective during inflationary periods, historic cost accounting is based on the accruals system. Capital values are subtracted to reflect the value of any expenses which will last longer than the accounting period. Depreciation is then added back as an amount estimated to equal the amount of 'capital' used during the period. Adjustments to the costs of purchases are also made if the closing stock is higher than the opening stock, to reflect the fact that this extra amount is available for consumption in the next period.

Current cost accounting addresses itself to four main areas. The first consideration is with items relating to fixed assets, the revaluation of assets to current values, and extra depreciation. Secondly, inflation has a major effect on the value of stock, consequently requiring cost of sales adjustments and allowance for stock uplift. The third area relates to adjustments in monetary working capital, more especially figures for debtors and creditors. The final area, and possibly the most important in terms of effect on shareholders' returns, is adjustment to gearing, i.e., the balance between debt and equity finance.

The overall effect of the adjustments is that the amount of capital employed increases through revaluation of stock and fixed assets. Equity increases in value through revaluation of reserves, resulting in lower gearing. Profit figures will generally be seen to fall because of increases in the cost of sales and depreciation resulting in a lowering of margins. Finally, speed of utilisation will fall because the capital employed has a higher value. The ratios shown in Table 1 will normally be lower if made according to CCA as opposed to historic cost accounting.

The function of financial management cannot be constrained to current profitability; it must also examine the claims to any funds generated and the patterns and likely trends in cost components in order to see the future in a proper perspective.

CONTROL OF COSTS

The measurement of productivity highlights the dangers involved in ratio analysis. The process attempts to identify the extent and cause of productivity changes, and four main practical difficulties emerge. The first involves the separation of commercial and technical productivities. The normal technique to measure outputs in a multi-product firm is to use a monetary measure; this immediately introduces marketing and pricing decisions. Secondly, the accruals system of accounting attempts to apportion capital throughout its life. Any change in capital input thus causes a problem of evaluating the contribution of capital of any one accounting period. Thirdly, unless labour productivity is measured according to skill groups, changes in the mix of skilled and unskilled labour may go unnoticed. The final problem involves the actual production process itself, in that quality may be changed or materials used may be substituted without being highlighted in the analysis. The solution of these problems requires an understanding of the company's operation and hence should present no significant problem to the exercise of internal control.

Meaningful measurement of productivity requires price changes to be removed from the calculations. This is normally achieved by revaluing factors of production and the product at constant prices. There is a further problem, with no easy solution, in deciding whether to use prices in the base year or current year when making an historical comparison.

The overall measure of trends in costs comes from the ratio:

$$\frac{\text{Cost of sales}}{\text{Net sales}}$$

This ratio can then be examined more closely in the light of ratios measuring the costs attributable to the main inputs, including labour, capital and administrative costs.

The difficulties in measuring productivity have been mentioned earlier in this section. The measurement of the performance of labour in terms of profit must be seen in the light of the remuneration to the workforce, hence two key ratios in this area are:

(a) Added value per employee $= \dfrac{\text{Gross profit}}{\text{Average number of employees}}$

(b) Remuneration per employee $= \dfrac{\text{Wages for the period}}{\text{Average number of employees in the period}}$

It may well be that performance of labour in these terms has increased by, for example, 10% but if remuneration has increased by 15% it could swallow much of the improvement in added value.

The ratio of administrative costs to sales is calculated as:

$$\frac{\text{Administrative costs}}{\text{Sales}} \times 100\%$$

A significant feature in this ratio is the denominator because many of the elements in administrative costs will be only semi-variable with sales (e.g. rent, rates, insurance). Consequently a fall in this ratio may well be caused by an increase in sales. The efficiency of the administrative process is reflected either through a fall in costs or through increased utilisation of the existing facilities in higher sales. Caution is important, in that poor administrative support could result in an increase in bad debts, lost business and goodwill and poor operational checking procedures. In the same way that overall costs can be broken down, administrative costs can sometimes usefully be subdivided into component parts.

Many control of cost ratios are covered within the study of management accounting and it is not intended to go into further detail here. The control of funds will require an investigation of many of the ratios covering the costs associated with capital.

CONTROL OF FUNDS

Control of short-term funds

The long-term survival of a company requires effective management of current funds. A company faces considerable risk if it reaches a situation where it cannot readily convert sufficient assets into cash in order to meet current liabilities. Several ratios provide indicators of a company's overall liquidity. Consideration of liquidity must be seen in two dimensions: firstly, the time required to convert an asset into cash; and secondly the certainty of realising any asset value. The overall structure of current assets includes components which may not readily realise the value to the company if they were to be sold on an open market, especially at short notice. Consequently, examination of liquidity requires consideration of the components of working capital.

A test of liquidity frequently applied is the *current ratio:*

$$\frac{\text{Average current assets for the period}}{\text{Average current liabilities for the period}}$$

Higher ratios supposedly indicate a greater ability to pay bills. Rules of thumb can be misleading in financial analysis; however, a frequently stated norm for the current ratio is 2:1. In other words, current assets need to be approximately twice the current liabilities to satisfy any potential supplier of credit. A ratio at this level also gives a picture of the company's financing policy, in that only 50% of current assets are financed by short-term finance which involves the company in the risk of not being able to replace repaid funds. Caution must be applied to the use of a norm of 2:1; however, there is considerable support for this approximate measure in that current assets include stocks which may not readily be converted to cash, but equally the ratio should not be high because current liabilities are a relatively cheap source of finance.

Stock can be removed from the numerator in order to give a more stringent measure of the ability to pay creditors in the short term. This ratio is sometimes referred to as the *acid test:*

$$\frac{\text{Average quick assets for the period}}{\text{Average current liabilities for the period}}$$

This is also known as the *liquidity* or *quick* ratio. Quick assets include cash and debtors and securities which can be quickly turned into cash.

The two ratios dealing with corporate liquidity, i.e., the acid test and the current ratio, face two basic constraints. Short-term loans are a relatively cheap source of credit, thus keeping the ratios low provides a framework for reducing the company's cost of capital. However, there is an opposite pressure to keep the ratios up because providers of finance will be anxious to see that there is good asset cover for the credit they provide. The ratios themselves do not provide information on alternative borrowing possibilities that are held in reserve.

The other components of working capital can usefully be examined through the use of ratios which will indicate any potential weaknesses in a company's financial management. Chapter 11, on working capital management, will highlight the importance of effective credit control, and the *debtors to sales* ratio attempts to indicate how much of a company's resources are tied up in its credit policy. This ratio:

$$\frac{\text{Debtors at end of period} \times \text{Number of working days in period}}{\text{Sales turnover in period} \times \text{Number of working days in year}}$$

must be seen in the light of the industry norm. The level of debtors is a consequence not only of credit control but also sales and marketing strategy and the nature of the industry.

Ratios relating to stock are also dependent on the type of operation the company carries out. However, industry comparison and historical trends can give useful insights into company control. The overall ratio for stock turnover includes work in progress (it is possible to exclude WIP):

$$\frac{\text{Cost of sales for period} \times \text{working days in year}}{\text{Stocks plus WIP at end of period} \times \text{working days in period}}$$

The numerator deals with the number of days in the year in order to give a figure of how many times the stock is turned over in any one year.

EMPIRICAL EVIDENCE

The application of financial ratios is commonplace, but that alone does not provide justification for their use. Financial reporting makes use of ratios in presenting data in a simple format for the reader of accounts, but this is not necessarily a major contribution to the management of business finance. Data are needed which aid decision-making, hence the ultimate test of a ratio's usefulness comes from its ability to predict future events. Two studies, one in the USA and another in the UK, provide examples of the usefulness of financial ratios.

E. I. Altman in a study of bankruptcy in America established a model, on the basis of five ratios, for predicting the likelihood of corporate collapse. (E. I. Altman 'Financial ratios, discriminant analysis and the prediction of corporate bankruptcy', *Journal of Finance*, September 1968.) The initial study examined 33 manufacturers who during the period 1946-65 had filed for bankruptcy in the USA. Companies of similar size and operation that had not failed during this period were then paired with the 33 in the sample. Starting with 22 potentially helpful variables selected on the basis of popularity in the literature and potential relevance, Altman used discriminating analyses to narrow the field down to five variables as doing 'the best overall job' of predicting failure. The five ratios derived were:

R_1 Working capital/Total assets
R_2 Retained earnings/Total assets
R_3 Earnings before interest and tax/Total assets
R_4 Market value of equity/Book value of debt
R_5 Sales/Total assets

The model stemming from these ratios is used to compute a Z score which is then used to predict the likelihood of business failure:

$$Z = 0.012R_1 + 0.014R_2 + 0.033R_3 + 0.006R_4 + 0.010R_5$$

This reinforces the need to examine liquidity ratios in a dynamic context, in that a company generating profits may be able to overcome short-term liquidity difficulties. Intuitively, common sense suggests profitability is an important factor and indeed the most useful ratio in the model is the 'current profitability' ratio R_3.

Altman's model gave correct predictions in 94% of the bankrupt cases and in 95% of all cases. Investigation of the individual ratio movements prior to bankruptcy corroborated the model's findings that bankruptcy can be accurately predicted up to two years prior to failure. This has considerable implications for auditors in suggesting the relative ease of establishing the need for qualifications to statements on a going-concern basis.

Taffler and Tishaw carried out a similar study in the UK, again using discriminating analysis to establish the significant ratios for the model. (R. Taffler and H. Tishaw 'Going, going, gone — four factors which predict', *Accountancy*, March 1977, pp. 50-4.) They argued that 'one of the most difficult decisions the auditor has to make is whether his client is or is not a going concern', and consequently a technique of predicting potential bankruptcy is a most useful tool. Linear discriminant analysis was applied to 80 different ratios in two groups, one set based on firms failing and the other on financially sound companies. The set of ratios that discriminated best between the two sets of firms produced the following model for quoted companies:

$$Z = K_0 + C_1R_1 + C_2R_2 + C_3R_3 + C_4R_4$$

Where

K_0 = a constant

$C_1 \ldots C_4$ = the ratio weights

R_1 = Profit before tax/Current liabilities

R_2 = Current assets/Total liabilities

R_3 = Current liabilities/Total assets

R_4 = 'No-credit' interval

The Z score ranks firms in increasing order of solvency. Taffler and Tishaw argue that there is a cut-off point and a position below this point indicates that a company's future survival is in danger. A company's presence on the list of low Z scores does not mean that it will fail, for this rests on the actions of creditors, of the government and, to a certain extent, of management.

It is interesting to note that the UK study came up with 'profit before tax/current liabilities' as providing over half of the model's discriminating ability. Once again the significance of a ratio indicating a company's ability to cover its current liabilities through its earning power is highlighted. Profitability, measured in different ways, is important to both the American and UK models.

The models described above have come under criticism, not least because the predictions are of companies *likely* to fail and do not pinpoint those that *will* fail. The extent to which Z scores become self-fulfilling prophecies may make an interesting future study.

4   Capital and money markets

NATIONAL INCOME ACCOUNTING

The economy can be divided into four sectors for national income accounting purposes:

(a) the business sector;
(b) the public sector;
(c) the personal sector;
(d) the overseas sector.

The funds flow between these sectors is aided by the activities of financial intermediaries. Flow of funds accounting at the national level is an extension of national income accounting. National income accounts are in effect the country's profit and loss accounts. Funds flow statements are produced showing, for each sector, where its funds came from and how they were used, thereby indicating the extent of interdependence of the sectors. The level of savings in each sector and where the savings are invested is vital for the health of the business sector and the economy.

Samuels and Wilkes in *Management of Company Finance* 3rd ed. J. M. Samuels and F. M. Wilkes, Nelson 1980 illustrated the flow of funds between sectors by the diagram shown in Figure 1.

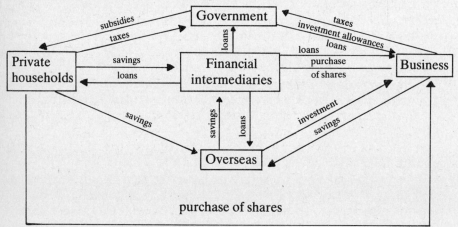

Figure 1   Flow of funds between sectors

National income accounts can be divided into two elements, current accounts and capital accounts. Current accounts cover day-to-day transactions. The current account of the business sector is merely a summary of the profit and loss accounts of business. The capital account includes expenditures where the resulting benefits are to be received in the future, such as investments in fixed assets, financial assets, etc.

THE FUNCTION OF FINANCIAL INTERMEDIARIES

The function of financial intermediaries is to transfer funds from people with an excess of money (surplus units) to those who require extra funds to fulfil their expenditure or investment plans (deficit units). The intermediaries act as channels for savings to pass into investment, and without them many of the funds in the economy would remain unused. The return or benefit for the intermediaries is gained as they make money by lending at a higher rate than that at which they borrow: the margin is intended to cover costs and, often, to make profits, or both, depending upon the extent of competition in the particular market.

The question which is often raised is why cannot the surplus and deficit units deal directly with each other without having to go through a financial intermediary? By cutting out the middleman, so to speak, they would cut costs as the deficit units would pay at a lower rate and the surplus units would obtain a higher rate. If the price of finance were the only criterion and if the finance market were sufficiently well organised, this would be possible, but deficit units and surplus units have divergent needs. The former often need to obtain long-term funds to finance risky fixed investment, whereas surplus units — often individuals — generally prefer that their savings should be safe, liquid and growing. Here lies the importance of the intermediary organisation, which acts to meet these divergent needs by making available to deficit units long-term finance which has been obtained from surplus units anxious to keep their savings safe. The way in which the intermediary is able to meet these divergent needs and consequently facilitate the flow of funds can be explained by examining what is involved in the process of transferring funds.

Individuals would often prefer *not* to acquire primary claims by investing in real capital goods, but they are willing to acquire secondary claims and therefore approach financial intermediaries to purchase bank deposits or bonds. At the same time companies often like to borrow from banks or other institutions rather than accommodate the often distinctly specific preferences of the investing public.

We may define primary securities as financial claims upon those engaged in the trading and manufacture of current output or equity capital issued by financial institutions. Secondary securities are created, on the other hand, when financial intermediaries issue claims upon themselves to finance such activity. The intermediation occurs as financial institutions buy primary debt issued by corporate, personal, or public borrowers, and in turn issue their own secondary securities to be held by non-financial lenders, mainly householders. Thus the flow of funds is facilitated by financial intermediaries because they transform primary debt into secondary securities.

The financial intermediaries are also able to operate and meet the divergent needs as they facilitate what is known as a 'liability transformation effect' and an 'asset transformation effect'.

Liability transformation effect

This relies on the law of large numbers and the presumption that it is unlikely that many small savers will, collectively, wish to withdraw their savings at once and unpredictably. Individuals may indeed do so, but the effect of their action will be limited and may be offset entirely by new deposits from other savers. Building societies are therefore able to accept deposits which are withdrawable without notice, and lend them on mortgages of up to 30 years. Thus the aggregate of savings with such intermediaries is more stable and predictable than the behaviour of the account of an individual saver might imply.

Asset transformation effect

Although a saver may want liquidity, he may also want to see his savings grow, and this will usually mean some loss of liquidity and the acceptance of some risk. It is here that financial intermediaries are able to use the asset transformation effect, through diversification and portfolio decision.

TYPES OF INTERMEDIARY

There are two identifiable types of intermediary in the financial system:

(a) Primary intermediaries: that is, those that issue securities directly to surplus spending units and purchase securities directly from deficit spending units, e.g., a building society issues shares and deposits to savers and makes loans directly to borrowers in the form of mortgages.

(b) Secondary intermediaries: these issue securities primarily to other financial intermediaries. Thus an insurance company, because it invests in stocks and shares, is acting as a secondary intermediary. The distinction is concerned with the contact between savers and borrowers: if this contact is one step removed or shared in any way by a number of institutions then they are regarded as secondary.

Earlier we defined a financial intermediary as an institution which issues financial claims on itself to surplus units in order to obtain funds either to purchase other financial claims or to lend directly to deficit units. This role of a financial institution is distinct from that of a bank which acts primarily as a repository for cash transactions, creating further cash for transactions where necessary. Ascheim (1961) expressed the distinction in the following terms: 'commercial banks are *creators* of loanable funds, whereas financial intermediaries are *brokers* of loanable funds'.

Yet banks do involve themselves in intermediation. The intermediation undertaken by banks, however, has declined relative to that by non-banks since the war. The rate of growth in banking activity has lost ground compared with the non-banks for the following three reasons:

(a) The commercial banks are heavily constrained by regulations which have tended in the past to apply only to banking activities.

(b) The banks have traditionally regarded the intermediaries as insignificant competitors.

(c) The amount of debt issued by governments has increased enormously in the past decade. The intermediaries have been active in taking up this increased debt, using the funds obtained from savers. An increasing public sector borrowing requirement therefore invites the growth of non-bank intermediaries.

There are a number of operational distinctions between non-bank intermediaries and banks.

First, non-bank intermediaries tend to cater for specific needs in the economic system. They have acquired considerable expertise in the gathering and interpretation of the information required to fulfil their own particular function. This information concerns the identification of surplus and deficit units in the economy and enables them to act as catalysts by which the transfer of funds may take place. In this capacity the intermediaries are effectively supplementing the market and ironing out inefficiencies in the system, which facilitates exchange. It is only relatively recently that the commercial banks have diversified their own activities either by direct expansion or by acquisition of existing intermediaries. Yet, although the commercial banks are sophisticated organisations, the intermediary function often requires specialised knowledge and personal contacts which take time to develop. Thus in 1980 the share of the personal deposit market held by commercial banks was as low as 34%.

A second distinguishing characteristic is that in general the lending activity of the non-banks is extremely restricted. For example, under the Building Society Act 1962 these institutions may only lend by way of mortgage on property, although this role is changing. Moreover, the role of reserves is quite different between banks and non-banks. Intermediaries can lend money subject to the constraint of a minimum liquidity ratio which is required for contingent withdrawals, whilst banks' reserve ratios are stipulated by the monetary authorities and hence their reserves are traditionally held by the intermediaries and the banks should be comparable either in size or content, because they fulfil different roles for each institution.

The aim of the regulations imposed upon the listed banks is not primarily to safeguard the interests of savers, which is a secondary consideration, but to create the appropriate economic climate through monetary policy. The regulations imposed on bank activities are aimed at controlling the supply and direction of money by controlling the lending activity of the banks. The banks argue that this directs money away from them to non-banks but while this is true, it is also true that money is created in this way. The Radcliffe Committee (1959) therefore proposed that monetary policy should seek to control the monetary supply and the liquidity of the non-banks. Monetary policy, it was argued, must operate on two closely related planes: one whereby the money creation by the banks is controlled, and a second whereby the liquidity and therefore the credit creation ability of the non-banks is similarly restrained.

We can distinguish between the banks and non-banks not only on functional grounds but also on the grounds that non-banks create financial instruments varying in liquidity whereas banks create money. It is the fact that the banks' financial liabilities are accepted as the final settlement of a debt that provides the greatest theoretical distinction between them and the non-bank financial intermediaries.

BANKING INTERMEDIARIES

Banks and discount houses

The role of banks has developed from being a depository for valuables to that of general deposit-taking institutions, thereby enabling an efficient means of payment to be established. Within the banking sector the discount market plays an important and unique role. The discount houses were originally established before the days of national commercial banks and their primary function was to provide a link between regional banks in different areas. This was developed, until now the discount houses act as 'banker to the banks'. The discount houses provide an important mechanism which enables the banks to convert excess into earning assets.

Investment trusts and unit trusts

Investment and unit trusts are institutions to which people entrust their savings in order that they may derive the benefits of diversified wealth portfolio, economies in the purchasing and selling of financial assets, and the professional advice of the trustees.

Investment trust companies act as a means through which individuals obtain investments in both the UK and overseas at a cost less than they would incur if they acted independently. ITCs are joint stock companies and as such they can issue both equity and prior charge capital. The overriding advantage of investment trusts is that they offer the investor an equity share in a 'geared' fund which is spread both geographically and industrially. The objective of a trust has been stated by the Association of Investment Trust Companies as follows: 'to provide shareholders over the medium- to longer-term with a secure and increasing return both in income and capital terms on their investment'.

The investor in an investment trust does not buy the underlying assets of the trusts as in the case of the unit trust, but holds shares in the company. Operationally an investment trust cannot hold more than 15% of the value of its investments in unlisted company securities and it own ordinary capital must be listed on the Stock Exchange as with any other company. Investment in any one company is restricted to 10%. Investment trusts are also restricted to a retention ratio of 15% of their income in any accounting period.

Unit trusts are similar to ITCs in that they raise capital in the savings market in order to invest in a portfolio of investments. There are, however, certain essential distinctions between the two institutions. First, their investment portfolios differ in that unit trusts tend to invest almost entirely in equities. Second, unit trusts are 'open-ended', which means that a person may invest in the trust or liquidate his holdings at will. Third, unit trusts cannot issue preference or prior charge capital except for foreign currency loans.

Unit trusts, unlike larger institutional investors, tend to devote a significant proportion of their investment to small and medium-sized companies where growth prospects may be encouraging but risks are correspondingly greater. They seek to achieve their objectives of increasing the unit-holders' investment and providing a steady flow of income by maintaining frequent contact with the companies in which they have invested.

Specialist intermediaries

Specialist intermediaries exist in the public and private sectors catering for the needs of industrial, commercial and personal borrowers and investors not adequately provided for by the other institutions we have discussed.

Public sector A public sector specialist is Investment in Industry (3i), formerly known as Finance for Industry (FFI), which is the holding company for the Industrial and Commercial Finance Corporation (ICFC) and Finance Corporation for Industry (FCI). The share capital of 3i is held by the Bank of England and the London and Scottish Clearing Banks but it still has sufficient independence to exercise complete discretion in the granting of finance and applies the normal criteria.

In 1975 the National Enterprise Board (NEB) was set up to provide equity and loan finance to ailing firms, predominantly in manufacturing. It must be noted that this has been reduced dramatically over the past few years.

Private sector   There are a number of specialist private sector institutions which cater for specific financial needs, examples being leasing and factoring companies. Others include those providing a personal financial planning service such as Plan Invest Group (PIG).

ROLE OF INSTITUTIONS IN CAPITAL MARKETS

There is a great deal of contemporary interest in the growth and power of financial institutions. One aspect of their development which is particularly subject to comment is their increasing presence in the stock market. This presence is especially apparent in the market for ordinary shares where insurance companies, pension funds, investment trust companies and unit trusts have significantly and persistently increased their holdings in UK quoted equities.

The rapid growth of institutional investors has been accompanied by increasing requests to institutional investors to involve themselves in managerial decision-making. The degree and nature of institutional activity that has been suggested varies enormously, from protector of the small investor to social responsibility within the firm. Although in the past institutional investors have played a minimal role in management their continued growth makes it inevitable that they will involve themselves in current management.

INSTITUTIONS AS A SOURCE OF FUNDS

The growing commitment of financial institutions to those companies in which they invest presents management with the opportunity to tap those major shareholders as sources of funds. The new issues market is a source of funds but only a small quantity is raised this way. On the occasions when firms do go to the stock market for equity finance, financial institutions are active in taking up rights issues and in placings.

Although there is a general lack of interest in new equity finance, financial institutions are capable of providing many forms of loan finance, including: secured and unsecured loans, arrangements for sale and leaseback, debentures and preference shares, provision of instalment credit, etc.

GOVERNMENT INTERVENTION

The NEB mentioned earlier provides an example of direct intervention by government where it has felt that the existing financial framework has not been adequate to provide necessary funds for what were considered socially desirable projects.

Government influence on the flow of funds to the industrial and commercial sector is threefold:

(a) As a major borrower itself, it competes with other sectors in the economy for funds.

(b) Through its various tax measures it affects the ability of commercial organisations to generate funds internally.

(c) It has in recent years taken on the role of financial intermediary.

A more complete analysis of the role of government in the financial framework is made in Chapter 2 on government action.

THE STOCK MARKET: ITS INSTITUTIONS AND DEALINGS

There are two types of market:

(a) a primary market, where new financial claims are issued;

(b) a secondary market, where previously issued financial claims are traded.

The stock market is both a primary capital market in which companies and other institutions can raise funds by issuing shares or loan stock, and also a secondary market for existing securities.

The initial sales of securities are made either through the agency of issuing houses or by stockbrokers. The subsequent transactions in the securities take place in the secondary market, the Stock Exchange.

THE STOCK EXCHANGE

Historical background

Since the seventeenth century the Stock Exchange has provided a market in which the goods bought and sold are stocks and shares. Initially transactions were facilitated by merchants and stockbrokers meeting together in coffee houses in the City of London. Stocks traded were mainly UK government stocks issued after the formation of the Bank of England in 1694; the trading of securities in the Hudson Bay Company and the East India Company also took place but the major impetus for the formation of the Stock Exchange came from the existence of large quantities of government stock issued during the wars of the eighteenth century. As the demand for shares did not always meet the supply of shares it became necessary for some intermediary to be willing to hold the surplus shares until a ready market developed. These intermediaries were stockjobbers.

By the early nineteenth century the volume of trading was such that it was necessary to house the Stock Exchange in a purpose-built building. Membership was limited and rules were drawn up to regulate the activities of members.

Stock Exchange institutions

The Stock Exchange has a governing body — a council — whose role is to ensure that members obey the rules, to decide on which companies to admit to a listing on the Exchange, checking that they meet the solvency requirements of the Exchange and to consider acceptance of new members or expulsion of old.

Until 27 October 1986 the London Stock Exchange operated on a single capacity system. Under a single capacity system there is a division of labour between jobbers and brokers. In other countries the tasks of jobbers and brokers are carried out by the same individuals and since the above date the London Stock Exchange has operated a dual capacity system.

Brokers

A member of the general public who wishes to buy or sell securities on the UK Stock Exchange must do so through the agency of a stockbroker, who will buy from or sell to a jobber. In return for his services the stockbroker will charge his client a commission. The commission charged by brokers varies with the value of the purchase or sale.

Jobbers

The jobbing system developed in the eighteenth century because of an imbalance between the demand for and the supply of shares. In the single capacity system which operated jobbers were willing to hold shares at times when other operators within the markets were anxious to sell their shares. As the number of jobbers was large, competition was assured. It is this competition between jobbers which led to the view of the Stock Exchange as one of the best examples of a perfect market. Each jobber held a set of securities from within a particular section of the market and brokers who wished to deal in a particular security went to the appropriate section of the market and bargained with the various jobbers in that section until they got the best deal for their clients. The jobber in effect matched buyers with sellers. If there were more sellers than buyers, the surplus shares would be held by the jobbers who would probably reduce their selling and buying prices in order to find buyers for any excess holdings. On the other hand, if demand for a share exceeded the current supply, jobbers could raise their buying prices so as to bring the market back into equilibrium. The jobbers earned their living by relying on the profit made in selling stock at a price higher than that at which they bought. In order to make a profit jobbers had to avoid holding either too much stock or selling more stock than they possessed. Accordingly, they adjusted their bid (buying price) and offer (selling price) to anticipate the reactions of investors. Most obviously this occurred when, say, unexpectedly large profits were announced by a company: jobbers tended to raise their quotation to avoid having to sell abnormally large amounts of shares to investors who now assessed the shares as being 'cheap' in relation to the previously quoted price. Similarly, it was common for jobbers to mark down their prices for a wide range of shares on the receipt of news which was expected to depress the profitability of British companies.

The marking up or down of prices by jobbers went some way towards maintaining their profitability but if it was insufficient, the jobber had to ensure a larger profit by widening the spread of 'turn' between the bid and the offer. The overwhelming problem for jobbers was that of financing the 'book' of securities in which they traded. Jobbers were able to finance part of their book of securities by borrowing from banks, but the need for capital remained, because the loans were not for the full value of the securities pledged as collateral. The shortage of capital meant that jobbers could only hold a restricted book, and this led to the situation in which many of the large deals of the institutions had to be arranged outside the Stock Exchange and then be 'put through'. It is evident that jobbing firms have experienced severe financial difficulties to the extent that many have merged, thereby reducing competition. A hundred firms existed in 1960 compared to 17 in 1984. The problems, mentioned above, were encountered by the jobbers and their methods of dealing have been changed by the move to a dual operating system in October 1986, whereby the functions of jobbers and brokers are no longer separated. This move, known as the 'Big Bang', is discussed at a little more length later in the chapter.

The share dealing mechanism

The conduct of business between brokers and jobbers can be illustrated by the following example.

Example A private investor wants to buy 2,000 shares in a listed company and instructs his brokers to buy shares on his behalf. They will approach a jobber and ask the buying and selling prices of those shares. The jobber will not know whether these brokers wish to buy or sell and must therefore quote two prices, for example 64-67p. Here the jobber is offering to buy shares in the company at 64p and sell them at 67p. The broker may then approach another jobber selling the same shares and ask for another quotation, although it must be noted that many shares are dealt with by one jobber only. The broker will then announce his intention of buying 2,000 shares at 67p each and the contract is settled.

When a deal is reached between broker and jobber to buy shares a contract note will be sent the following day to the broker's client (the investor), giving details of the securities bought and their cost, the transaction costs, and settlement day.

An investor can delay payment by a mechanism known as 'contango', by which payment is delayed until the next settlement day on payment of 'contango interest'. This is only possible, however, if the buyer is able to find a seller willing to accept deferral of payment.

Brokers and jobbers were strictly segregated in the single capacity system. Operation on such a system effectively protects the interests of individual investors, but this strictly single capacity system has changed somewhat (as discussed above) as brokers and jobbers are now not strictly segregated. Brokers are able to deal in shares on their own behalf, thus cutting out the role of jobbers. Now that firms of brokers and jobbers have merged, brokers can deal directly in shares using the experience of a jobbing concern to provide the expertise needed. It must be noted, however, that there is an inherent danger in this changed system that brokers will not find the best share prices for clients, and might even seek to profit from selling clients shares that they deal in and so profit from them themselves.

Speculation

The Stock Exchange year is divided into 24 time periods called 'accounts'. Each account begins on a Monday and ends on a Friday. Settlement day is the Tuesday 11 days after the end of the account in which the purchase note has been agreed and the contract note sent. This means there will be a lapse of two to four weeks between the deal being agreed and payment being due. This dealing mechanism means that it is possible to buy and sell shares many times during the course of an account, but the only payment to be made is for transactions outstanding at the end of the account. This delay allows for speculation.

Bulls   A person who buys securities in the hope that the price will rise before he must pay, enabling him to sell at a profit without ever taking up the shares.

Bears   A person who sells shares he has not got, in the hope that the price will drop before he has to deliver the shares to the buyer. If prices do fall he will be able to acquire the shares he must deliver at a lower price than that at which he sold.

UNLISTED SECURITIES MARKET

In its early days the USM was crowded with speculative oil exploitation stocks and young high-tech companies, not all of which were of the highest investment quality. Since its beginnings, however, the USM has grown in a variety of ways.

During 1985 the number of companies quoted passed the 300 mark for the first time and by the beginning of 1986 the market consisted of more than 340 companies with a combined worth of £3.5 billion. There is now also a greater variety of company; the USM's old dependence on oil and high-tech companies has gone, with less than a fifth of the latest entrants coming from these sectors. Of the new companies entering the USM a large number are food companies and there is also an onslaught of 'people businesses' (such as advertising, marketing and public relations), creating two thriving USM subsectors.

In its early days the USM provided immodest profit for stags, i.e., speculators who apply for new issues in the hope of selling any allotments at a profit when dealings commence rather than making a long-term investment, but this has long ceased to be the norm. On the evidence of recent USM flotations, sponsors are getting better at pricing issues whilst investors are becoming more careful in making their assessment of newcomers. One-third of last year's issues managed to achieve a premium of between 5-15% for their sponsors whilst 12% of companies suffered their shares opening at a discount to their issue price.

In 1985 it was pleasingly evident that companies are putting the market to better use than before — raising more money to expand their businesses, and making greater use of their shares for acquisitions. USM companies made more than 60 acquisitions last year, many of which were for shares. In total, one in every five USM companies has at some stage made use of its paper to make an acquisition.

The USM is still a volatile place for investors; 20% price movements in the space of a week are not uncommon. In 1985 47 shares fell by more than half and 14 companies saw their shares rise by more than 100%. The market as a whole ended the year only 2% higher than at the outset, and the Datastream USM index rose from 112 to only 115. It can be noted, however, that, ignoring the electronics shares, the index advanced by 16%.

1985 saw the collapse of electronics shares on both the USM and the major market. The USM electronics sector fell by nearly 50%. The effect of this has been to lessen the USM's dependence on electronics stocks.

Finally, as far as the future is concerned, there is some concern with regard to the effect of the 'City revolution' on the USM, i.e., the effect of the introduction of dual capacity and the scrapping of minimum commissions. The concern is that this will concentrate market resources on larger companies, making dealings in shares of smaller ones — never liquid at the best of times — dry up altogether. Some believe this may deter institutions from investing in the USM, leading to a fall in prices and deterring companies from joining the market. Others argue, however, that with most of the large share transactions already being matched by the sponsoring broker and a small role already being played by the jobber, the City revolution may not have an adverse affect on the USM.

OPTION DEALINGS

An option is the right to buy or sell shares at a known determinable price within a stated period. At present it is possible to deal in two different types of option on the Stock Exchange: (a) negotiated options; (b) traded options.

Negotiated options

Negotiated options are arranged individually for the investor by his stockbroker. They may, theoretically, be for any number of shares for any period of time, although in practice most negotiated options are for three months. An investor may acquire: a call option, which means he is entitled to acquire the shares at the stated price within the specified period; a put option, which means he has the right to sell the shares at the stated price within the specified period; or, if he is thoroughly undecided, he may take a two-way option, which gives the right to buy or sell.

The cost of a negotiated option is usually between 5 and 10% of the price of the shares at the time the option is taken out. The advantage of an option is that the investor can, if his prediction of the share price movement is correct, reap a large return for a small initial cost.

Traded options

Options offer their holders the right to buy (call options) or sell (put options) shares at a fixed price at some time in the future, usually within a few months, normally three. There is a distinction between European options with a fixed term and American options which can be exercised any time throughout the period of contract.

The obstacle to the success of options appears to be lack of investor understanding of options — in particular, perhaps, private investors who consider options too risky an investment. This concept of options as particularly risky and speculative investments is not a recent one. Dealing in options was officially banned on the London Stock Exchange from 1734 to 1860 and again from 1939 to 1958.

Also, the major difference between traded options and the types of securities we have considered so far is that options do not represent direct claims on the assets of the borrower. An ordinary shareholder holds the right to some fraction of the earnings and assets of the company, whereas a call option holder merely has the right to buy shares in the future, representing only a potential claim on the company's assets. An ordinary shareholder holds a security issued by the company, providing funds for the company in return for future income. A traded option holder has no relationship with the company whose shares he has an option to buy or sell. He has simply entered into an agreement with another party, the option seller or 'writer', concerning possible future share transactions between the option holder and the option 'writer' at a predetermined price.

Options are speculative investments, but the investor can vary the risk element in shares in both directions; that is, the investor may either increase or decrease expected return and risk by trading in options. By simultaneously holding shares and writing call options on those shares, he can reduce his risk to less than that of simply holding the shares.

The purchase of a *call* option on an ordinary share entitles the holder to buy the share, on or before some fixed date in the future, at a fixed price. The fixed date is known as the exercise or expiry date and the fixed price is known as the exercise or striking price. A *put* option, on the other hand, entitles the holder to sell an ordinary share on or before the expiry date at a fixed price. Puts or calls which offer the holders the option to exercise *before* as well as on the expiry date are known as American options. European options entitle the holders to exercise their options to buy or sell only *on* the expiry date itself. Traditionally, in the UK, options were of the 'European' type. However, the traded options market has been based on the US options markets, and so traded options purchased on the UK Stock Exchange are of the 'American' type.

The *Financial Times* produces daily information on London traded options.

The value of a call option

The value is determined by two factors:

(a) The current market price at the expiration date, MV
(b) The exercise price EP

$$V = MV - EP$$

Thus if a share at the exercise date has a market price of £5 and an exercise price of £4 it would be worth £1 to obtain the option, V must be positive otherwise an investor would simply purchase the share in the market. The wealth position of the investor is determined by how much he originally paid for the option and the time value of that money.

Hedging

An investor holding shares in a company can balance his expectations of a
possible fall in share prices by taking out an option to sell at a fixed price at
some future date. The investor has now eliminated risk and would therefore
anticipate a return similar to the risk free rate.

F. Black and M. Scholes, 'The pricing of options and corporate liabilities'
Journal of Political Economy, May-June 1973 used this risk free position of a
hedged portfolio to determine the value of an option when the market is in
equilibrium. Essentially the value of an option is seen as an increasing function
of the time to exercise date, the risk free rate of return and a measure of
variability of the rate of return on the shares. The model assumes no
transaction costs, no dividends during option period and the efficient market
hypothesis at the weak level. The increasing use of computers makes the
application of this complicated model much more feasible.

THEORIES OF SHARE PRICE BEHAVIOUR

Chartists

Chartists attempt to predict share price movements by assuming that past price
patterns will be repeated. There is no real theoretical justification for this
approach, but it can at times be spectacularly successful. Critics of charting
suggest that it is so unscientific as to be of no practical value. Against this must
be set the point that charting is concerned with share prices. The price of a
company's shares is the most up-to-date information about it. Furthermore,
the price can be considered as reflecting the collective wisdom of all investors
and potential investors and their advisers.

The efficient market hypothesis

It has been argued that the UK and US stock markets are efficient. The essence
of an efficient stock market is that in which any information relevant to a firm is
fully and immediately absorbed in its share price.

Capital market efficiency has been defined in three forms, each specifying a
different interpretation of the influence of eligible information.

(a) *Weak form efficiency* This describes a situation where excess or
abnormal returns cannot be earned on the basis of historical price or returns
information. This argues that the historical pattern of prices or returns on
stocks will not provide a basis for superior forecasting of future prices or
returns. This contradicts the arguments of the chartists which suggest that by
observing the pattern of price or returns behaviour some trading rules can be
developed for achieving superior performance.

(b) *Semi-strong efficiency* The semi-strong form of the efficient market hypothesis states that all publicly available information will be reflected in current share prices. Thus any new, publicly accessible information should be accurately and immediately reflected in current share prices. Consequently, investment strategies based on such public information should not enable the investor to earn abnormal profits because these will have already been discounted by the market.

(c) *Strong form efficiency* This asserts that any information, whether public or not, is immediately and accurately reflected in market prices.

If the efficient market hypothesis is correct, a company's real financial position will be reflected in its share price. Its real financial position refers to both its current position and also its expected future profitability in the case of the semi-strong form and more especially so for the strong hypothesis.

Share prices are related to interest rates so that if the stock market displays a semi-strong or strong form of efficiency one might conclude that share prices would rise in anticipation of a fall in interest rates; if the stock market displays a weak form of efficiency one might conclude that share prices would not rise until the fall in interest rates had actually happened.

RECENT DEVELOPMENTS

The 'big bang'

'The government decided in 1983 to withdraw a reference of the Stock Exchange's practices to the Restrictive Trade Practices Court, on condition that fixed commissions would be abolished by the end of 1986. Major changes have flowed from that decision. On 27 October this year [1986] (the day of the 'big bang') fixed commissions will be abolished, and dual capacity permitted — the same firm will be allowed to act both as principal on its own account and as agent for its clients.

'Full ownership of Stock Exchange firms by non-members has been permitted from 1 March this year, opening the way for the new financial conglomerates, which include clearing banks, merchant banks, brokers and jobbing firms, now preparing to operate in the market after October. Banks, both British and foreign, will become more involved in the London securities markets.

'Until this year, the Stock Exchange has consisted of some 5,000 individual members in some 200 firms, mainly partnerships, organised on the basis of strict separation between a few jobbers, acting on their own account, and many more brokers, acting as agents for investors and dealing with the jobbers on their client's behalf. Pressure for change has become more insistent as market integration has proceeded worldwide, and advanced information technology has made possible more or less instant dealing across the globe. Freedom to compete and adapt, and in particular to join large groupings which can provide the necessary capital, have become essential to participants in the London market.

'After 27 October all firms, whether market makers or not, will be able to act in dual capacity. In the equity market some broker dealers will be registered market makers, required to maintain firm two-way quotes for deals of normal market size (probably 1,000 shares) on an electronic quotation dissemination system (Stock Exchange Automated Quotations — SEAQ), so ensuring a continuous market in the shares with which they are concerned. There will also be other broker-dealers, not required to maintain a continuous market and without certain privileges, for example in the use of SEAQ. Deals will not be conducted through SEAQ, but over the telephone, or on the floor of the Stock Exchange.

'Similar arrangements, based on market makers responsible for sustaining a continuous market in return for a dealing relationship with the Bank of England and the use of certain facilities, will prevail in the gilts market.

The impact of technology

'The changes taking place in financial markets have been made possible only by far-reaching developments in technology. The Clearing House Automated Payment System (CHAPS) was set up by the UK banks in 1984. SEAQ has already been mentioned. The Stock Exchange set up its automated securities settlement system — Talisman — in 1979; it is now being adapted to offer settlement facilities for both UK and overseas securities, and it will be able to deal with settlements under dual capacity once this comes in. Links are to be developed with overseas organisations, likely to lead towards a worldwide integrated network, bringing almost instantaneous trading worldwide and around the clock.

'Some brokers are developing their own systems, while others will use settlement agencies.

'The Bank of England and Stock Exchange joint project for computerised settlement of transactions in gilt-edged securities was inaugurated in January, with the introduction of a Central Gilts Office service. The service is to be enhanced by the provision of assured payment facilities when the new market structure for gilts is introduced in October.

'In April the Stock Exchange announced it would be setting up a small order automatic execution facility (SAEF), expected to reduce substantially the costs which have long been a major discouragement to small investors contemplating share buying. Initially the facility, which should be available some time in 1987, will handle transactions of up to 1,000 shares (which account for 40 per cent of the current number of bargains).'

Source: *Economic Progress Report,* July 1986,
Publications Division, Central Office of Information

These changes have necessitated a review of the supervision of the capital markets. The Financial Services Act 1986 provides the most comprehensive overhaul of investor protection legislation for over 40 years. The Bill gives the Trade and Industry Secretary of State powers to authorise and regulate investment businesses and the ability to transfer many of these powers to designated agencies. The policy is one of 'self-regulation within a statutory framework'.

The process of improving efficiency within the capital market by reducing transaction costs and improving information flows has been reinforced by the recent reductions in stamp duty.

A new source of finance

'On 20 May [1986] the first issues in the UK of sterling commercial paper were made. These are debt securities, issued by major companies whose shares are listed on the London Stock Exchange, with a maturity of at least seven days but under a year. Before then companies were only able to issue commercial paper abroad, notably in the well-established US market or in the growing Eurocommercial paper market. This was because they were prohibited from directly raising short-term sterling finance under the Banking Act 1979, which restricted deposit-taking to banks and similar institutions. They have now been exempted from this provision and are able to issue commercial paper denominated in sterling.

'This innovation represents an extension of the financing options open to major industrial and commercial companies. They can now raise short-term finance in the market on the strength of their own creditworthiness, as an alternative to bank borrowing or the raising of funds through bank acceptances such as commercial bills.'

Source: *Economic Progress Report,* July 1986,
Publications Division, Central Office of Information

5 Sources of long-term finance

Organisations need long-term finance to finance long-term projects, fixed assets, etc., whereby repayment is not required for at least 10 years, if ever. Long-term finance takes a variety of forms but there are three main types of investment:

(a) *Variable income and capital investments* The most important type of investments with variable capital and income are ordinary shares.

(b) *Fixed income investments (loan capital)* These will normally have a nominal value which will be the amount payable on redemption, and their market value will vary with current interest rates. Examples include debentures, preference shares, etc.

(c) *Fixed capital investments* The investor deposits a sum of money, normally for a period of time, on which he receives interest. Examples include commercial bank deposits, local authority loans, unquoted government bonds, etc.

The terms 'source of finance' and 'investment' may be used interchangeably. To clarify this it must be noted that a source of finance to an organisation is also an investment to an investor. We are looking from the viewpoint of the firm, therefore we are looking at sources of finance rather than investments in this chapter.

EQUITY: NEW ISSUES

The new issue market is a primary finance market because it is concerned with the creation of new financial claims. As we noted in the preceding chapter, it provides a method which may be used by deficit units to raise funds from surplus units. In Britain it is controlled by the London Stock Exchange and is closely related to the secondary trading market run by the Exchange.

A company seeking to obtain additional equity funds may be: an unquoted company wishing to obtain a stock market quotation; an unquoted company wishing to issue new shares but without obtaining a stock market quotation; a company which is already listed on the Stock Exchange wishing to issue new shares.

In the Stock Exchange the new issues must carry with them a 'listing' on the trading market; and a minimum of 35% of the company's market capitalisation must be offered to the market by the first issue of shares. A company seeking a listing must be represented by a stockbroking member of the Stock Exchange. The timing of an issue has to be cleared with the Bank of England, if it is for more than £3 million, in order to ensure that announcements of new issues do not coincide, that the liabilities of the underwriters to this and other issues are not excessive and that the closing date of the issue and the date of the first dealing on the trading market are 'reasonably spread'.

In making an issue, a company usually enlists the aid of an issuing house, and the issue must be sponsored by a member of the Stock Exchange. Applications for a listing on the London Stock Exchange have to be accompanied by a prospectus drawn up according to the rules of the Stock Exchange.

The Stock Exchange Council requires that all companies seeking a listing on the UK Stock Exchange should speedily disclose any new information regarding acquisitions, new operations abroad and changes in the character of the operations of the company which may lead to stock market price changes. The ultimate sanction of the Stock Exchange for a breach of this requirement is the suspension of dealing.

There are six different methods of issuing shares available to companies in Britain.

(a) *Public issue by prospectus* By this method the company, through the agency of the issuing house, seeks to persuade the public to buy a large number of shares in the company by means of an advertisement in two London newspapers. The main difference between the public issue by prospectus method and the offer for sale is that in the former case the issuing house acts as the agent for the issue of shares whereas in the latter case it acts as the principal.

In most cases it is illegal to issue to the public any form of application for shares or debentures in a company unless it is accompanied by a prospectus complying with the Companies Act 1985, or approved listing particulars or a statement of where approved listing particulars may be inspected. The prospectus must include an accountant's report and a report on the value of business to be purchased.

(b) *Offer for sale* This method is used when a relatively large amount of capital is required and often when a company wants to change its status to that of a public company. The company offers shares to an issuing house, which then offers the shares to the public at a fixed price. The procedure for making an offer is as follows:

(i) Application to publish a prospectus must be made to the Committee on Quotations of the UK Stock Exchange.

(ii) Once the prospectus has been published at least two days must elapse before a formal application for a quotation is made to the Stock Exchange

Committee on Quotations. The application list for the shares will open on a date stated in the prospectus.

(c) *Private placing* This method is used by unquoted companies who require a small amount of funds and wish to keep the expenses of the issue as low as possible. Either the issuing house or a firm of stockbrokers will agree to buy a small number of the securities of the company with the intention of placing them with some institutional investors. It is usually the intention to have the shares quoted on the London Stock Exchange at some time in the future.

(d) *Stock Exchange introduction* This form of issue is different from all other methods of issue in that no extra capital is raised. The real function of an introduction is to make it possible for a firm to obtain a quotation on the UK Stock Exchange. After the introduction has been approved by the quotations subcommittee of the Stock Exchange and assurances have been given that there will eventually be a free market in the shares of the company, the introduction is advertised in the London daily papers.

(e) *Stock Exchange placing* This method is an amalgamation of the private placing and the Stock Exchange introduction. The company concerned will need both a quotation for its shares and a small amount of capital, which is usually raised from selected institutional investors.

(f) *Issue by tender* By this method shares are offered to the public and potential investors are invited to name the price they are willing to pay. Though the company does not suggest or even know the price at which the shares will ultimately sell to the bidder, it does put a reserve on them — the minimum price below which they will not be sold. The investor therefore knows the lowest selling price and can, if he wishes, make an offer above this level.

Example If a company offers 15,000 shares to the public and 15,000 investors offer £0.50 or more for the shares, then all the shares will be sold if the price is set at £0.50. It is possible that, in total, 30,000 investors offered £0.40 or above for the shares, but the 15,000 who offered between £0.40 and £0.50 will not receive an allocation. The shareholder does not necessarily have to pay the price he offered for the shares: 1,000 of the investors may have offered as much as £1 for the shares, but they will only have to pay a price of £0.50 per share because this was the price which cleared the issue. It must be noted that the Stock Exchange will not allow a multi-tiered price structure — only one striking price is allowed.

Underwriters

In the case of offers, an issuing house acts as the principal and buys the shares from the company before the issue is made. In all other methods of issuing shares the merchant bank or issuing house acts as the agent for the issue of shares. Irrespective of whether the issuing house is acting as the principal or merely the agent for a new issue of shares, it will be facing a business risk because it guarantees that the money will be raised. To cover itself it arranges with a number of other financial institutions, such as investment trusts or insurance companies, that they will underwrite the issue. These institutions are paid a fee which is forthcoming even if the issue is fully subscribed. In addition, the institutions carrying out the underwriting facility will have the opportunity of obtaining some cheap shares.

Costs of flotation

Two important points can be made about flotation:

(a) The cost of flotation for ordinary shares is greater than for fixed interest stocks.

(b) The cost of offers for sale as a percentage of gross proceeds is greater than the cost of placings.

One reason for the greater expense involved in marketing ordinary shares lies in the fact that fixed interest securities are generally bought in large blocks by a relatively few institutional investors, whereas ordinary shares are bought by large numbers of individuals. Similarly, ordinary shares are more volatile than fixed interest securities, so underwriting risks are greater for the former.

Costs also tend to be greater, as a percentage of total proceeds, for small issues, such as placings, than for large issues, such as offers for sale. There are two explanations for this. First, certain fixed expenses are associated with any issue of securities; since these expenses are relatively large and fixed, their percentage of the total cost of flotation runs high on small issues. Second, small issues are typically those of less well-known firms, so underwriting expenses may be larger than usual because the danger of omitting vital information is greater.

Flotation costs are lower for larger companies for each type of security and most companies can cut their flotation costs by making full use of rights issues (see below) as a method of issuing new securities.

UNLISTED SECURITIES MARKET

Obtaining a Stock Exchange quotation involves a large dilution of equity and considerable financial cost; consequently many companies are reluctant to seek a quotation. A number of years ago, therefore, an investment banker called M. J. H. Nightingale set up an over-the-counter market for unlisted securities. This prompted a response from the stock market, which set up a mechanism for dealing in unlisted securities under the Stock Exchange rules, no. 163, and then finally, in 1980, set up its own market in unlisted securities.

The rules of the USM are considerably more relaxed than for a full Stock Exchange listing and consequently it fills an important need for medium-sized unlisted companies.

RIGHTS ISSUES

If a sale to existing shareholders is made this is known as a rights issue. Each existing shareholder is given an option to buy a certain number of the new shares. Each shareholder receives one right for each share he holds. The number of shares he is offered is determined by the percentage of his existing share ownership in relation to the total number of company shares.

It is often argued that rights issues will depress the price of the existing ordinary shares of the company. To the extent that the rights price is lower than the current market price the effect on the market price of the ordinary shares will be similar to that experienced when a company makes a bonus issue.

Factors in making a rights issue

When considering a rights issue the company must decide how much it wants to raise and how many shares to issue and therefore the price of each share. The way in which these factors are dealt with can be explained by two examples.

Example 1   How much to raise   The balance sheet of Eggshell Ltd is as follows:

	£		£
Ordinary shares: 3,000 at £1 nominal value	3,000	Assets	9,000
Retained earnings	2,000		
Debentures (10%)	4,000		
	9,000		9,000

The net asset value per share is £1.67 (= £5,000/3,000).

The company is earning approximately 20% on its existing total assets made up as follows:

	£
Total earnings	1,840
Interest	400
	1,440
Tax (50%)	720

Earnings per share is £0.24 (= £720/3,000).

The possible capital issues and their resulting returns are as below:

New funds (£)	Expected net returns (£)	Average rate of return on new investments (%)
2,000	300	15
3,000	360	12
4,500	405	9

The market's rate of capitalisation for a company of this type is 12%; this is the required earnings yield, and is equivalent to a P/E ratio for the company of 8.33:1.

If the market behaved rationally, valuing the company on the capitalised earnings of the firm at the market's normal rate of capitalisation for a firm of this type, the total value of the company before the issue would be £710/0.12 = £6,000.

After raising £3,000 the value would be: £1,080/0.12 = £9,000.

Raising this amount of capital satisfies the constraint that the earnings from the new issue must be sufficient, when capitalised, to increase the market value by the amount of the new funds. This would not have been the case if £4,500 had been raised.

The amount of funds that should be raised by a new rights issue is therefore dependent on the earnings of the company on these new funds, and the rate at which the market capitalises earnings for such a company.

Example 2   Pricing the rights issue   Having determined the amount that can be raised from a rights issue, it is necessary to determine the number of shares to be issued, and to decide on their price.

Fast Lane Ltd can achieve a profit after tax of 20% on the capital employed. Its current capital structure is:

	£
400,000 ordinary shares of £1 each	400,000
Retained earnings	200,000
	600,000

It is proposed to raise an extra £300,000 from a rights issue. The current market price is £1.50 per share. The company in setting a rights issue price must ensure it is sufficiently low to secure the acceptance of shareholders but not so low as to create an excessive dilution in earnings per share. In order to calculate the 'best' rights price we need to calculate the number of shares which need to be issued at various prices and the dilution of earnings per share at each price.

The earnings at present are 20% of £600,000 = £120,000. This gives earnings per share of £0.30. The earnings after the rights issue will be 20% of £900,000 = £180,000.

Rights price (£)	No. of new shares (300,000/price)	EPS (180,000/ total no. of shares)	Dilution
1.40	214,285	29.3p	0.7p
1.20	250,000	27.69p	2.31p
1.00	300,000	25.71p	4.29p

The number of shares resulting from a £1.00 issue price results in a 14.3% dilution of earnings.

Advantages of rights issues

The pre-emptive right gives the shareholders the protection of preserving their share in the ownership and control of the company. Their earnings are also safeguarded.

Advantages to the firm are also evident. By offering new issues of securities to the existing shareholders, it increases the likelihood of a favourable reception of the new shares. The flotation costs of rights issues are also lower than those for offers for sale. The Stock Exchange estimates that the average cost of rights issues is 4.1% compared with 7.6% for offers for sale.

The company may also obtain positive benefits from underpricing. Since a rights issue is similar in some ways to a bonus issue, it will cause the market price of the shares to fall to a level lower than it would otherwise have been. However, rights issues may increase the number of shareholders in a company by bringing the share price to a more attractive trading level.

Finally, the total effect of a rights issue may be to stimulate an enthusiastic response from shareholders and the investment market as a whole, with the result that opportunities for financing become more attractive to the firm.

Theoretical ex-rights price

The value of rights is the expected or theoretical gain a shareholder would make by exercising his rights. The value of a right is determined using the following formula:

$$\text{Value of rights} = \frac{\text{Market price (ex-rights)} - \text{Rights price}}{\text{No. of shares needed to give right to 1 new share}}$$

Example   Foodfare Ltd has 100,000 £1 ordinary shares in issue, which have a market price on 1 September of £2.10 per share. The company decides to make a rights issue. The shareholders are given the right to buy one new share at £1.50 each for every four shares already held. After the announcement of the issue the share price fell to £1.95, but just prior to the issue being made, it had recovered to £2 per share.

The theoretical ex-rights price is calculated as follows:

	£
100,000 shares (at £2) have a cum rights value of	200,000
25,000 shares (at £1.5) will be issued to raise	37,500
	237,000

The theoretical ex-rights price is £237,000/125,000 = £1.90 per share.

ORDINARY SHARES AS A SOURCE OF FUNDS

An equity interest in a company may be said to represent a share of the company's assets and a share of any profits earned on those assets after other claims have been met. The equity shareholders are the owners of the business; they purchase shares, the money is used by the company to buy assets, the assets are used to earn profits which belong to the ordinary shareholders.

As a source of long-term finance ordinary shares carry a number of both advantages and disadvantages for a company.

Advantages

(a) There are no fixed charges attached to ordinary shares. If a company generates enough earnings it will be able to pay a dividend but there is no legal obligation to pay dividends.

(b) Ordinary shares carry no fixed maturity.

(c) They provide a cushion against losses for creditors, thus the sale of ordinary shares rather than other securities increases the creditworthiness of the firm.

(d) Ordinary shares can often be sold more easily than debentures.

(e) Returns from the sale of ordinary shares in the form of capital gains are subject to capital gains tax rather than corporation tax.

Disadvantages

(a) The sale of ordinary shares extends voting rights or control to the additional shareholders who are brought into the company.

(b) More ordinary shares give more people the right to share with the existing owners in the company's profits.

(c) The costs of underwriting and distributing new issues of ordinary shares are usually higher than those for underwriting and distributing preference shares or debentures.

(d) If the firm has more equity or less debt than is called for in the optimum capital structure the average cost of capital will be higher than necessary.

(e) Dividends payable to ordinary shareholders are not deductible as an expense for the purposes of corporation tax but debenture interest is deductible.

SCRIP DIVIDENDS AND SCRIP ISSUES

One way of issuing new equity shares to existing shareholders is by the distribution of a scrip dividend. As an alternative to paying out cash dividends during the year, a company may choose to pay a scrip dividend. This is essentially a transfer to the shareholder of a number of additional equity shares without the shareholder having to subscribe additional cash. From the company's point of view this offers the advantage of preserving liquidity, as no cash leaves the company. The advantage to the shareholder on the other hand is that he receives a dividend which he can convert into cash whenever he wishes through selling the additional shares. These dividends have been taxed in the same way as cash dividends since 1975.

A scrip issue is similar to a rights issue, however shareholders do not have to take up the additional equity. A company uses its capital reserves through a capitalisation of its share premium account.

STOCK SPLITS

A stock split, like a scrip dividend or issue, increases the number of shares in a company without raising any new funds. The procedure is simple: the company reduces the nominal (par) value of each share, and announces that its investors no longer hold, say, one share with a par value of £0.50; instead they own two shares with a par value of £0.25 each. One of the prime objectives of a stock split is to create cheaper shares with increased marketability. If the marketability of the company's shares improves, the value of the investors' holdings should increase.

PREFERENCE SHARES

Preference shares usually have priority over ordinary shares with respect to earnings and claims on assets in liquidation. Preference shares are usually cumulative; some are redeemable and others are irredeemable. They are typically non-participating and have only contingent voting rights. The major advantages to the issuing company are:

(a) The obligation to pay a fixed rate of interest on the security is not binding in the same way as it is with debentures.

(b) Preference shares enable the company to avoid dilution of equity capital which occurs when additional ordinary shares are issued.

(c) They also permit a company to avoid sharing control through participation in voting.

(d) Since many preference shares are irredeemable, they are more flexible than debentures.

The major disadvantage is that dividends paid to preference shareholders are not tax-deductible, consequently the true cost to a company of preference shares is far greater than the cost of debentures.

As a hybrid security, the use of preference shares is favoured by circumstances that fall between those favouring the use of ordinary shares and those favouring the use of debentures. The costs of preference share financing follow interest rate levels more than ordinary share prices; in other words, when interest rates are low, the cost of preference shares is also likely to be low.

Companies sell preference shares when they seek the advantage of financial gearing but fear the dangers of the fixed charges on debt in the face of potential fluctuations in income. If debt ratios are already high or the costs of equity financing are relatively high, the case for using preference shares will be strengthened.

DEBENTURES

A debenture is a document issued by a company containing an acknowledgement of indebtedness. Usually a debenture is a bond, which is given to the public in exchange for money lent, and a prospectus must have been supplied with the application form. The company agrees to repay the principal to the lender by some future date, and in each year up to repayment it will pay a stated rate of interest in return for the use of funds. The debenture-holder is a creditor of the company, and the interest has to be paid each year before a dividend is paid to any class of shareholder.

Debentures and debenture stock can be secured or unsecured. When secured this is by means of a trust deed. The types of debenture are:

(a) *Mortgage debenture* This type of debenture is secured by means of a specific charge upon certain real assets of the company. A mortgage debenture is, therefore, secured by real property.

(b) *Debentures with a floating charge* These debentures are secured against all assets of the company other than those assets which have been charged in the form of mortgage debentures. Although the legal security of these debentures is less than in the case of mortgage debentures, the company does have greater flexbility in managing its assets. If the company defaults in the payment of interest the debenture-holders have the right to appoint a receiver to administer the assets until the interest has been paid or the default made good.

(c) *Unsecured debentures* These debentures have no security. The only security possessed by the debenture-holders is a note of indebtedness issued by the company.

As with ordinary shares, loan capital also carries a number of advantages and disadvantages.

Advantages

(a) The cost of debt is definitely limited. Debenture-holders do not participate in superior profits if earned.

(b) The expected yield is lower than the cost of equity capital.

(c) There is no dilution of equity capital and the shareholders do not have to share their control when debt financing is used.

(d) The interest payment on debentures is deductible as a tax expense.

Disadvantages

(a) Debt is a fixed charge.

(b) Higher risks bring higher capitalisation rates on equity earnings. Thus, even though gearing is favourable and raises earnings per share, the higher capitalisation rates attributable to gearing may drive down the market price of the ordinary shares.

(c) Debentures usually have a fixed maturity date. Because of this fixed maturity date, provision must be made for repayment of the debt.

(d) Since long-term debt is a commitment for a long period, it involves risk. During that time the debt may prove a burden, or it may prove to have been advantageous.

(e) There is a limit to the extent to which funds can be raised through long-term debt.

(d) Since many preference shares are irredeemable, they are more flexible than debentures.

CONVERTIBLE DEBENTURES

Convertible debentures are debentures that are exchangeable into ordinary shares at the option of the holder and under specified terms and conditions. The most important of the special features relates to how many shares a convertible holder receives if he converts. This feature is defined as the conversion ratio, which gives the number of shares the holder of the convertible receives when he surrenders his security on conversion. Related to the conversion ratio is the conversion price, or the effective price paid for the ordinary shares when conversion occurs.

The following terms are used in connection with convertibles:

(a) *Conversion price* This is the price at which stock may be converted into shares.

(b) *Conversion ratio* This is the number of shares for which each £100 of loan stock may be converted, and is simply another way of expressing the conversion price. If stockholders are entitled to 200 shares for every £100 of stock, the conversion price is 50p per share.

(c) *Conversion premium* The conversion price is always fixed at a figure above the market price of the shares at the time of issuing the stock. The conversion premium indicates the amount by which the current share price at the time of the issue of the convertible would have to rise to reach the conversion price. If at the date the stock is issued the share price is 40p and the conversion price is fixed at 50p, the conversion premium is 25%. This means that, if by the date at which conversion is permitted the market value of the shares has risen more than 25%, the stockholder can make a capital gain by converting his stock into shares at 50p, and selling the shares at the higher figure. Because a convertible gives the investor the potential of making a capital gain, companies can usually issue such stocks at a rate of interest lower than normal loan stock. How much lower depends on the likelihood of the stockholder making a capital gain, which in turn depends on the conversion premium. If the conversion price were set far above the market price of the ordinary shares at the time of issue, thus making a capital gain unlikely, then the company would have to offer an almost normal interest rate.

Provision is generally made for a change in the conversion ratio in the event of a bonus or a rights issue. If, for instance, the original conversion ratio is 150 shares for every £100 of loan stock and the company makes a 1 for 3 scrip issue, the market value of the shares will drop proportionately. To maintain the original value of the conversion terms, the ratio must be increased by ⅓ from 150 shares to 200 shares, since 200 shares after the scrip will have the same value as 150 shares before the scrip.

Every rights issue contains an element of scrip issue, since, as previously illustrated, the issue price has to be lower than current market value.

Example   Assume that a company which has 1,000,000 shares in issue, each with a market value of £2, wishes to make a rights issue at 160p to raise £200,000. This will entail issuing £200,000/160p = 125,000 shares. Such an issue could be looked on as:

100,000 shares at full value of £2	= £200,000
25,000 scrip issue	—
Total proceeds	£200,000

Out of the total of 1,125,000 shares, 25,000 would be the bonus or scrip issue, i.e., a ratio of 25,000 to 1,100,000 or 1 for 44. The conversion ratio of any convertible stock in issue would therefore have to be increased by 1 for 44.

Conversion value

The conversion value of a stock is obtained by multiplying the conversion ratio by the current share price. If an investor holds £1,000 of stock convertible at 50p, then he is entitled to 2,000 shares. If the shares are currently standing at 60p, then the conversion value of his stock is 2,000 × 60p = £1,200, and he has made a gain on his investment of £200.

The terms of conversion sometimes stipulate specific dates on which conversion may take place, or simply state a period during which the investor may convert. Obviously, if the share price does not rise sufficiently, the conversion value may be such that conversion is not worthwhile. If, in the above example, the value of the shares had dropped to 30p, the conversion value of the stock would be 2,000 × 30p = £600. The convertible itself, even though it bears a lower than average rate of interest, may be worth more purely as a loan stock, in which case the stockholders will not convert.

From the investor's point of view a convertible offers a fixed rate of interest with the chance of a capital gain, i.e., it has some of the elements of loan stock and some of ordinary shares. However, an investor cannot get the best of both worlds. While having the security of loan stock, he has a lower interest rate than on a non-convertible. Equally, if he does make a capital gain, it will be less than he could have made by investing in ordinary shares.

Example   S Limited issued a 6% loan stock redeemable in 19X0 but convertible into ordinary shares any time after 1 January 19X8 at 50p per share. Mr X invested £1,000 in the stock at the date of issue and by 1 January 19X8 the ordinary shares had risen from 40p, the price at 1 January 19X6 to 60p. His capital gain is as follows:

Number of shares received on conversion	$=$	$\dfrac{£1,000}{50p}$	$=$	2,000
Value per share at 1 January 19X8			$=$	60p
Value of holding	$=$	$2,000 \times 60p$	$=$	£1,200
Original investment				£1,000
				———
Gain				£ 200

However, had he invested his £1,000 in ordinary shares at 1 January 19X6, he would have made a gain as follows:

Number of shares obtainable for £1,000	$=$	$\dfrac{£1,000}{40p}$	$=$	2,500
Value of holding at 1 January 19X8	$=$	$2,500 \times 60p$	$=$	£1,500
Original investment			$=$	£1,000
				———
Gain				£ 500

On the other hand, had he invested his £1,000 in ordinary shares there is always the possibility of a severe drop in the share price and a capital loss. The investment in the convertible, however, will always be worth its value as a straight loan stock, no matter what happens to the price of the ordinary shares. Thus, for the investor the convertible, as regards risk and potential gains, represents a half-way house between ordinary shares and loan stock.

As it gives the holder the chance of a capital gain, a convertible loan stock can generally be issued at a lower than normal rate of interest. A company which intends raising funds in the form of ordinary shares can benefit from this by delaying the equity issue and issuing a convertible instead, thus having the advantage of cheap loan capital for several years. However, in return it has to offer the convertible loan stock holders the chance of eventually buying the company's shares at a bargain price. If, for example, a company issues £500,000 of 8% loan stock convertible at 50p when the current rate for ordinary loan stock is 10%, then it benefits by £10,000 p.a. in lower interest charges as long as the stock is outstanding. If, however, when the stock is eventually converted, the company's share price is 60p, then it has lost 10p per share in being committed to convert at 50p. In other words the company has to issue £500,000/50p = 1,000,000 shares to convert the loan stock instead of £500,000/60p = 833,333 shares.

If, however, the share price does not rise to 50p, the stock holders will not convert and the company will have had the benefit of the lower interest rate without giving anything away. Paradoxically, the more the company prospers and the higher its share price, the less it benefits from having issued the convertible with its fixed conversion price.

Both the company (representing existing shareholders) and the investors in the convertible stock are taking a gamble. If the share price rises very high, then the convertible stockholders win at the expense of the company. If the share price rise is modest, then the company wins at the expense of the convertible stockholders. However, most convertible stock are issued on a rights basis, so that to the extent to which existing shareholders are also convertible holders, the gains and losses cancel out.

To sum up, the convertible stock does not offer the subscriber or the issuing company any intrinsic advantages over other methods of fund raising, but merely offers each a different package or risk and potential return.

Market value of a convertible

A convertible is both a loan stock and an entitlement to shares and at any time the value of one of these will be higher than the other. The value of the convertible, however, should be above the higher of the two. Given a current interest rate of 10%, an 8% convertible with four years to redemption would have a value as a straight loan of £93.66, as follows:

PV of four interest payments at 10% = £8.00 × 3.17 = £25.36
PV of £100 in four years = £100 × 0.683 = £68.30 = £93.66

If it were convertible into 80 shares, each worth 150p, it would have a conversion value of £120. In fact, its market value would probably be above £120, since no matter what happens to the shares, it cannot fall below its loan value of £93.66. Investors will pay something extra for this safeguard. If, however, the shares were only worth 105p (i.e., the conversion value is £84), then the convertible would probably be valued at something above its loan value of £93.66 because of the possibility that the share price might recover and push the conversion value up again.

MEDIUM-TERM LOANS

Medium-term financing is defined as debt originally scheduled for repayment in more than one year but in less than 10 years. Anything shorter is a current liability and falls in the class of short-term credit, while obligations due in 10 years or more are thought of as long-term debt.

The major forms of intermediate term financing are: (a) term loans; and (b) lease financing.

Term loans

A term loan is a business loan with a maturity of more than one year. Repayment arrangements are negotiable, although the usual practice is for systematic repayments over the life of the loan. The majority of loans made by the clearing banks are made without any security being taken. Yet, where it is felt that the capital resources of a borrower are not considered adequate in relation to the level of borrowing to warrant lending on a totally unsecured basis, then security is taken, usually in the form of a fixed or floating charge over certain assets.

Lease financing

Leasing provides for the acquisition of assets and their 'complete financing' simultaneously. Leasing takes several forms:

(a) *Sale and leaseback*   Under a sale and leaseback arrangement, a firm owning land, buildings or equipment sells the property to a financial institution and simultaneously executes an agreement to lease the property back for a specified period under specific terms.

(b) *Operating leases* Operating leases include both financing and maintenance services. These leases ordinarily call for the lessor to maintain and service the leased equipment, and the costs of this maintenance are either built into the lease payments or contracted for separately. Operating leases are not fully amortised, i.e., payments are not sufficient to recover the full cost of the equipment. Also the operating lease frequently contains a cancellation clause giving the lessee the right to cancel the lease and return the equipment before the basic lease agreement expires.

(c) *Financial leases*   A strict financial lease is one that does not provide for maintenance services, is not cancellable, and is fully amortised. Financial leases are almost the same as sale and leaseback arrangements, the main difference being that the leased equipment is new and the lessor buys it from a manufacturer or a distributor instead of from the user lessee.

INTEREST RATES

The term structure of interest rates and the levels of interest rates are obviously of prime importance. We will consider first the nature of the different types of interest rates. The most commonly quoted interest rates in the financial markets are:

(a) the banks' base rate;
(b) the inter-bank lending rate;

(c) the Treasury bill rate;
(d) the yield on long-dated gilt-edged securities.

Other interest rates include those for bank overdrafts, bank deposit accounts, etc.

Until August 1981 the Bank of England's minimum lending rate was an important determinant of general levels of interest rates on the markets. It was the rate at which the Bank was prepared to lend to the discount houses as a lender of last resort. Raising or lowering the MLR was an instrument of government policy.

In August 1981, however, the government changed its policy of monetary control, and the way in which the Bank of England acted to raise or lower short-term interest rates. As a result of the new emphasis on open market operations by the Bank in the discount market, the MLR lost its significance as an interest rate.

The term structure of interest rates

The term structure of interest rates describes the relationship between interest rates and loan maturities. When measuring term structure it is common practice to use yields on British government securities.

Three theories have been advanced to explain the term structure of interest rates:

(a) *Expectations theory* The expectations theory asserts that in equilibrium the long-term rate is a geometric average of today's short-term rate and expected short-term rates in the future.

Example An investor is planning for two years in advance: let r = short-term interest rate and R = long-term interest rate. He has £100 and is considering two alternative strategies: (i) purchasing a two-year bond with a yield of 9% per year; or (ii) purchasing a one-year bond that yields 8% then reinvesting the £108 he will have at the end of the year in another one-year bond. If he chooses (i) he will have £100 + £9 + £9.81 = £118.81. If he adopts (ii) he will have:

$$£100 \,(1.08) \,(1 + r_2) = £108 \,(1 + r_2)$$

In equilibrium the two returns will be the same:

$$£108 \,(1 + r_2) = £118.81$$

$$1 + r_2 = 1.1001$$
$$r_2 = 0.1001 = 10.01\%$$

Thus the longer term 9% rate can be seen as an average of the current short-term rate and the expected short-term rate in 1 year's time.

Suppose the r_2 was greater than 10.01% — say 10.5%. In that case the investor would be better off investing short-term, because he would end up with £119.34.

(b) *Liquidity preference theory* The future is inherently uncertain, thus the pure expectations theory must be modified. In a world of uncertainty investors will in general prefer to hold short-term securities, because they are more liquid in the sense that they can be converted to cash without danger of loss of principal. Investors will therefore accept lower yields on short-term securities. Borrowers will react in exactly the opposite way from investors — business borrowers generally prefer long-term debt because short-term subjects a firm to greater dangers of having to refund debt under adverse conditions. Accordingly, firms are willing to pay a higher rate, other things held constant, for long-term funds than for short-term funds.

(c) *Market segmentation theory* This theory admits the liquidity preference argument as a good description of the behaviour of investors with short horizons. Yet certain investors with long-term liabilities might prefer to buy long-term bonds because, given the nature of their liabilities, they find certainty of income highly desirable. Borrowers typically relate the maturity of their debt to the maturity of their assets. Thus the market segmentation or hedging pressure theory characterises market participants as having strong maturity preferences, then argues that interest rates are determined by supply and demand in each segmented market, with each maturity constituting a segment.

Each of these theories carries some validity, and each must be employed to help explain the term structure of interest rates.

6 *The cost of capital*

The cost of capital is the rate of return a firm must earn on its investments for the market value of the firm to remain unchanged. It can also be thought of as the rate of return required by the market suppliers of capital, which a firm must comply with in order to attract necessary financing at a reasonable price. Acceptance of projects with a rate of return below the cost of capital will decrease the value of the firm; acceptance of projects with a rate of return above the cost of capital will increase the value of the firm. The objective of the financial manager is to maximise the wealth of the firm's owners. Using the cost of capital as a basis for accepting or rejecting investments is consistent with this goal.

RISK

A basic assumption of traditional cost of capital analysis is that the firm's operating and financial risk are generally unaffected by the acceptance and financing of projects.

Operating risk is related to the response of the firm's earnings before interest and taxes (operating profits) to changes in sales. When the cost of capital is used to evaluate investment alternatives, it is assumed that acceptance of the proposed projects will not affect the firm's operating risk. However, the types of projects accepted by a firm can greatly affect its operating risk. If a firm accepts a project that is considerably more risky than average, suppliers of funds to the firm are quite likely to raise the cost of funds. This is because of the decreased probability of the fund suppliers receiving the expressed return on their money. Nevertheless, in analysing the cost of capital it is assumed that the operating risk of the firm remains unchanged.

Financial risk is affected by the mixture of long-term financing, or the capital structure, of the firm. Firms with high levels of long-term debt in proportion to their equity are more risky than firms maintaining lower ratios of long-term debt to equity.

We will now consider the costs of specific sources of capital.

EQUITY CAPITAL

Equity holders invest in shares in the expectation of obtaining returns in the form of dividends and/or capital gains. There are only two ways of providing further equity finance:

(a) new equity issues;
(b) retentions of profits.

New issues

A new issue of shares will normally be made only if the returns from this issue would be such that share prices would increase. If share prices were expected to fall as a result of a share issue, thereby reducing shareholder wealth, then the shares would not be issued. Therefore, it can be said that the *minimum* return required from a new issue is that which would leave the share price at its present level.

In the absence of any issue costs or changes in investors' attitudes towards the organisation, this return would be the rate at which the market capitalises future earnings — which in practice means the current return obtained from the existing shares.

There are a number of valuation models which can be used.

Dividend valuation model

If the future dividend per share (d) is expected to be constant in amount then the ex-dividend share price (MV) is calculated by the formula:

$$MV = \frac{d}{(1+r)} + \frac{d}{(1+r)^2} + \frac{d}{(1+r)^3} + \ldots$$

where r = the shareholders' marginal rate of time preference or cost of ordinary capital.

$$\frac{1}{(1+r)} + \frac{1}{(1+r)^2} + \frac{1}{(1+r)^3} + \ldots = \frac{1}{r}$$

So $MV = d \times \dfrac{1}{r}$ and therefore

$$r = \frac{d}{MV}$$

By this valuation method, the equity cost of capital would be defined as the minimum rate of return (including a risk allowance) that must be obtained from a project to ensure the maintenance of the value of existing equity.

The dividend valuation model is based on certain assumptions:

(a) No issue costs are incurred.

(b) Dividends from projects for which the funds are required will be of the same risk type or quality as dividends from existing operations currently in progress.

(c) All shareholders have perfect information about the company's future.

(d) Taxation can be ignored.

(e) All shareholders have the same marginal rate of time preference and the costs of borrowing and lending are the same.

Relaxation of assumptions   The assumption that no issue costs are incurred is not realistic, and adjustments would be needed in practice. It should be clear that extra returns would be needed to cover issue costs. Further, the assumption that investors would put an organisation into the same risk category both before and after the change in equity may not be valid, as additional projects may be considerably more risky, and investors may well add a larger risk premium to their required rate of return in order to compensate for additional risk. This can lead to extremely high marginal costs of equity and must be incorporated in the decision-making process. It can also be noted that the assumption of perfect information is unlikely to be true in practice.

Relaxation of these assumptions poses problems for the calculation of the cost of equity capital, and results will not be as easily or as precisely obtained as the model perhaps implies.

Dividend growth model (Gordon's model)

A further problem in calculating the cost of equity is that shareholders often expect dividends to increase year by year, and not to remain constant in perpetuity. As the theory of share values states that the market price of a share is the discounted future cash flows of returns from the share, the market value, given an expected growth in dividend, would be:

$$P_0 = \frac{D_0(1+g)}{(1+K_D)} + \frac{D_0(1+g)^2}{(1+K_D)^2} \cdots + \frac{D_0(1+g)^n}{(1+K_D)^n} + \cdots$$

where P_0 (ex div) is the current market price
D_0 is the current dividend (net of imputation tax)
K_D is the shareholders' marginal rate of time preference (i.e., IRR and the company's cost of equity)
g is the expected annual growth in dividend payments

This equation can be simplified to:

$$P_0 = \frac{D_0(1+g)}{K_D - g}$$

$$P_0(K_D - g) = D_0(1+g)$$
$$P_0 K_D - P_0 g = D_0(1+g)$$
$$P_0 K_D = D_0(1+g) + P_0 g$$

Dividing equation by P_0 gives:

$$K_D = \frac{D_0(1+g)}{P_0} + g$$

Estimating the growth rate   If we are to calculate the cost of capital using Gordon's model, we must first calculate g, the average growth rate. The following example illustrates how to estimate the growth rate.

Example 1   Over the last five years the earnings and dividends of Walton Franks Ltd have been as follows:

Year	Dividends £	Earnings £
19X1	160,000	400,000
19X2	195,000	510,000
19X3	210,000	550,000
19X4	240,000	650,000
19X5	266,000	700,000

It must be noted that Walton Franks Ltd is financed entirely by equity; there are 1,000,000 shares in issue, each with a market value of £3.35 ex div.

The growth rate can be estimated using the historic growth in dividends. Dividends over four years (19X1-X5) have risen from £160,000 to £266,000. The average growth rate (g) may be calculated as follows:

Dividend in 19X1 $\times (1 + g)^4$ = Dividend in 19X5

$$(1 + g)^4 = \frac{\text{Dividend in 19X5}}{\text{Dividend in 19X1}}$$

$$= \frac{266{,}000}{160{,}000}$$

$$= 1.662$$

$$\therefore 1 + g = (1.662)^{1/4}$$

The fourth root is the square root of the square root, i.e.:

$$1 + g = \sqrt{(\sqrt{1.662})}$$
$$= 1.135$$
$$g = 0.135 \text{ or } 13.5\%$$

The historic growth rate 19X1-X5 is 13.5% and is assumed by shareholders to continue into the indefinite future. The cost of equity is therefore calculated in the following way:

$$\frac{D_0 (1 + g)}{P_0} + g$$

$$= \frac{0.26600 (1.135)}{3.35} + 0.135$$

$$= 0.225 \text{ or } 22.5\%$$

The cost of equity (or the rate of return on new investments) is 22.5%.

The rate of growth of dividends can also be estimated on the basis of the likely return to be achieved on any retained earnings. This return could then be used to increase dividends in the future. Gordon expresses this formula as:

$$g = r.b$$

where g = growth rate of dividends
       b = rate of retention of earnings
       r = return on capital employed

Example 2

Dividend payment 28.2.19X6: 20p
Share price 6.3.19X6: £2.20
Historic rate of growth of dividends is 10% p.a.

The equity cost of capital may be calculated as follows, using Gordon's model:

$$r = \frac{20(1+0.1)}{220} + 0.1 = 0.2$$

Cost of equity is 20%.

Example 3 A plc, a listed company engaged in the manufacture of woollen goods, has an issued capital of 500,000 ordinary shares of £1 each. It has no fixed interest capital. The company has recently held its annual general meeting at which accounts were presented showing after tax earnings of £450,000. In accordance with this company's practice, one third of this is distributed as dividend. Profits have been growing at an average rate of 5% p.a. and this trend is likely to continue for the foreseeable future. A copy of the profit and loss account is given below. Today's market price for A plc's shares is £5.16 cum dividend.

The board will shortly announce plans for expansion involving capital expenditure of £210,000, expected to yield additional post-tax earnings of £60,000 in the current year, with the normal rate of growth thereafter.

At the moment alternative plans are under discussion for financing this expenditure. These are to make a rights issue at £4.20 per share of one new ordinary share for every 10 held, or to issue £210,000 12% debenture stock by a stock exchange placing.

A plc profit and loss account
year ended 30 September 19X1

19X0 £000		19X1 £000
8,430	Turnover	7,320
809	Profit before taxation	750
380	Taxation	300
429		450
4	Extraordinary items	(10)
433	Profit attributable to ordinary shareholders	440
143	Dividends proposed	150
290	Profit retained in the business	290

The cost of capital to the company at the present time can be calculated in the following way.

Since the finance structure is entirely equity, the cost is that of equity finance established using Gordon's model:

$$K_D = \frac{D_1}{P_0} + g$$

D_1 = expected dividend = 30p × 1.05
P_0 = current price (reduced to take account of declared dividend)
g = expected growth of dividends (5% in line with earnings)

$$K_D = \frac{0.315}{4.86} + 0.05 = 0.1148 \text{ or } 11.5\%$$

The theoretical justification for this approach is based on the dividend valuation model for shares, i.e.

$$P_0 = \frac{D_1}{(1 + K_D)} + \frac{D_2}{(1 + K_D)^2} \cdots + \frac{D_n}{(1 + K_D)^n} + \cdots$$

Thus £4.86 is the discounted value of the *future* dividend stream. The other £0.30 is the current dividend.

Criticisms of the dividend growth model   This model has been criticised by various writers on the following grounds:

(a)   It is difficult to visualise a situation where there are exactly the right number of projects available earning a given return to justify the use of a fixed proportion of earnings.

(b)   There is a strong argument that a future growth pattern is impossible to predict because it will be inconsistent and uneven.

(c)   The growth model should be based on expectations of *future* growth, but given uncertainty and imperfect information, investors must normally use records of historic growth in order to predict future growth, however inaccurately.

(d)   Gordon himself argued that an investor's uncertainty about dividend receipts in the future will become greater the further into the future he looks. To allow for the increase in risk with time, the investor will therefore apply a discount rate to expected dividends which increases year by year into the future. In other words, the concept of a single cost of capital for equity may not be valid.

The connection between retained earnings and growth is a critical assumption in the growth model. Shareholders *must* believe that retained earnings will result in future growth otherwise the model is invalid.

RETAINED EARNINGS

Retained earnings are the single most important source of finance to business organisations, particularly for purposes of expansion and growth.

Retained earnings have no direct cost but have a clear *opportunity cost*. If profits are paid out as dividends, shareholders can invest part or all of these dividends to make further returns. If profits are retained, the opportunity for shareholders to obtain such additional returns is eliminated. These forgone opportunities will need to be made up by the organisation in the form of future dividends or growth in share values. These internal returns should amount to at least as much as the returns potentially available from investment made outside the company.

DEBT CAPITAL

The cost of new debt can normally be calculated by reference to the interest rate payable. If £1 million of debentures are issued at par, with an interest rate of 10%, the before-tax cost of that debt would be 10% if transaction costs were ignored. If transactions (issue) costs are incurred, or debt is not issued at par, certain adjustments will need to be made.

The cost of debt capital already issued is the rate of interest (IRR) which equates the current market price with the discounted future cash receipts of the security. In the case of irredeemable debt (or preference shares) the future cash flows may be considered as the interest (or dividend) payments in perpetuity, so that:

$$D_0 = \frac{i}{(1 + K_D)} + \frac{i}{(1 + K_D)^2} + \frac{i}{(1 + K_D)^3} \cdots + \frac{i}{(1 + K_D)^n} + \cdots$$

where i = interest (dividend) received
K_D = the IRR, which is the cost of debt capital
D_0 = the current market price of debt capital after payment of the current interest (dividend)

Thus,
$$K_D = \frac{i}{D_0}$$

Example 4

19.3.19X6: £90 market value of debenture
Annual return on 6 March: £9

$$K_D = \frac{£9}{£90} = 10\%$$

Redeemable debentures

All UK debentures will be redeemed at par value. The return to the investor
has two sources: (a) interest; (b) repayment.

The IRR is established using the following formula:

$$R_0 = \frac{i}{(1 + K_r)} + \frac{i}{(1 + K_r)^2} + \cdots \cdots \frac{i + RV}{(1 + K_r)^n}$$

where R_0 = value of the debenture, current market value

         RV = redemption value n years from the date of current
                market value

         K_r = cost of redeemable debentures to the company in the
                absence of taxation

         i = interest payment, note, redemption is assumed to be the
                day after an interest payment.

THE WEIGHTED AVERAGE COST OF CAPITAL

The weighted average cost of capital is found by weighting the cost of each
specific type of capital by the *historical, target,* or *marginal* proportions of each
type of capital used.

When major capital projects are being evaluated, from the aspects of
expected costs and revenues, the cost of capital required to finance the project
will be a major cost. Often the capital to be employed will be a mix of newly
raised equity capital, at one cost, plus retained profits at a slightly lower cost
since no issue expenses would be incurred, plus long-term loans, assumed in
this case to be at a fixed rate of interest. When such a mix of components is
used, the cost of capital must reflect the cost of each component and the
proportion which each bears to the total of capital required for the project. A
'weighted average' is used since a simple average cost of capital would be inappropriate; thus, if there were more of a low-cost component the overall cost
of capital would be lower than it would be if more of a high-cost component
were used.

There are two possible approaches to the calculation of the weighted average cost of capital (WACC): either to weight the costs by the *book value* of the different forms of capital; or to weight them by the *market value* of each form of capital. The calculation of WACC using book values and market values is shown by the following example.

Example 5   GF Ltd has 20,000 ordinary shares, £6,000 in 15% loan stock, and £4,500 short-term loans on which the rate of interest is 9%. The book value of the ordinary shareholders' funds is £19,500. The market price per ordinary share is £2.50 and the loan stock stands at 104. The rate of corporation tax is 50%. The assumed cost of equity capital is 16% after tax.

Using *book value weightings* the weighted average cost of capital would be:

Form of capital	Book value (£)	Weighting (%)	Cost after tax (%)	Weighted cost* (%)
Equity	19,500	65	16	10.40
Loan stock	6,000	20 (50% × 15)	7.5	1.50
Short loans	4,500	15 (50% × 9)	4.5	0.68
	30,000	100		12.58

*Weighting × Cost after tax

If *market value weightings* were used the result would be:

	Market value (£)	Weighting (%)	Cost after tax (%)	Weighted cost (%)
Equity: 20,000 × £2.50	50,000	82.3	16	13.17
Loan stock £6,000 × 104	6,240	10.3	7.5	0.77
Short loans	4,500	7.4	4.5	0.33
	60,740	100.0		14.27

The market value approach is the more realistic, for the following reasons:

(a)   The 16% cost of equity capital was based in the first instance on studies of rates of return obtained by investing at market prices.

(b) Investments are normally rated by reference to their earnings yield, and the company has a responsibility to maintain that yield.

(c) At the present time the historical book values used in preparing balance sheets do not represent, or purport to represent, a valuation of the capital employed.

(d) In evaluating its own investment decisions, such as the purchase of new assets or the development and launching of new products, the business must look for a rate of return appropriate to the cost of the capital employed in the project.

It must be noted that although the cost of equity has been illustrated above at the figure of 16% which we assumed as an average cost for all companies, the percentage to be used when making a cost of capital study for a particular company will incorporate a risk rating relevant to the nature of the business, and the inflation percentage currently being experienced.

Example 6   Aston Ltd and Villa Ltd are two companies operating in the same industry. Each company had sales of £2,400,000 in 19X6 but, whereas Villa Ltd has an automated production process and uses high quality material, Aston Ltd uses a manual production process with inferior quality material. The following operating data for 19X6 in respect of each company are available:

	Aston Ltd	Villa Ltd
	£	£
Sales	2,400,000	2,400,000
Units sold	160,000 units	150,000 units
Direct material costs	900,000	975,000
Direct labour costs	600,000	225,000
Production overhead	200,000	500,000
Administrative and selling overheads	210,000	210,000
Interest on debentures	50,000	90,000
Tax rate	50%	50%
Ordinary dividend payout ratio	50%	50%
Price/earnings ratio	6	5

The following summarised balance sheets for the two companies are also available:

	Aston Ltd £	Villa Ltd £
Fixed assets	1,000,000	1,600,000
Current assets	1,500,000	900,000
	2,500,000	2,500,000
Capital:		
500,000 £1 ordinary shares	500,000	—
2,000,000 25p ordinary shares	—	500,000
200,000 10% preference shares	200,000	—
Sundry reserves	750,000	800,000
Debentures	400,000	600,000
Sundry creditors and accruals	650,000	600,000
	2,500,000	2,500,000

The WACC may be calculated in the following way:

Aston Ltd	Market value (W) (£000)	Dividend/ Interest (£000)	Cost (%)	WACC (%)
Ordinary shares	1,200	100	8.33	5.56
Preference shares	200	20	10.00	1.11
Debentures	400	25	6.25	1.39
	1,800			8.06

Note: Weights are found from the proportion of any single source of capital making up the total capital structure e.g., ordinary shares = 1,200/1,800 = ⅔.

Villa Ltd				
Ordinary shares	1,000	100	10.00	6.25
Debentures	600			2.81
	1,600			9.06

72   *The cost of capital*

It must be noted that although the two companies are operating in the same industry they are not subject to the same operating risk, i.e.:

Contribution per £1,000 of sales revenue:

Aston Ltd: $\dfrac{900}{2,400} \times 1,000 = £375$

Villa Ltd: $\dfrac{1,200}{2,400} \times 1,000 = £500$

Villa Ltd has greater operating risk than Aston Ltd and this is reflected in its higher costs of debt and equity.

Example 7 Spirax Holdings plc is a diverse group with interests in entertainment, property and machine tools. Its target capital structure is as follows:

	£million
Ordinary share capital	30
Retained earnings	75
Debt	45
	150

The company's share price is 120p and it has just paid a net dividend of 12p. Dividends and profits have been growing at 10% per year in money terms but a growth rate of only 3% is expected in the future as it is anticipated that inflation will fall to zero. Currently debt interest is 12% before tax and the corporation tax rate is 30%.

A new office block is expected to cost £4.5 million to construct and you can assume all this is to be spent at the end of 19X4. Rentals from the office block are forecast at £0.4 million per annum after taxation and these will be received at the end of each year for 50 years after construction is completed. The residual value of the building at that time is forecast to be £0.1 million. The project is to be initially financed by a bank loan costing 12% per annum repayable over 15 years.

The directors have been arguing amongst themselves as to what cost of capital to use in their calculation. The marketing director reckons it is the cost of the bank loan since that is the actual cost of funds used. The financial director argues for the weighted average cost of capital since he says that is the overall cost of funds needed. The planning director has a slightly different argument. He says it is the risk of the project that is significant and he reckons that property investment is really pretty low risk and a reasonable cost of capital would be a rate 1.5% above the post-tax cost of debt ($12\% \times (1 - 0.30)$) = 8.4%, say 10% post tax.

In order to calculate the WACC it is necessary to establish the component costs of capital and the weights.

(a) Components
Equity: established using Gordon's formula:

$$K_D = \frac{D_1}{P_0} + g$$

where K_D = cost of equity capital
D_1 = anticipated dividend
P_0 = current ex-dividend share price
g = anticipated annual growth in dividends

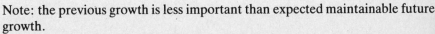

This gives:

$$\frac{12\,(1.03)}{120} + 0.03 = 0.133 \text{ or } 13.3\%$$

Note: the previous growth is less important than expected maintainable future growth.

Debt: established by taking the net current market rate for debt in this risk class, i.e.:

$$K_d = i \times (1 - t)$$
where K_d = cost of debt
i = current market rate of interest
t = company's marginal rate of tax

This gives:

$$12\,(1 - 0.30) = 8.4\%$$

(b) Weights
To establish the weights the target capital structure is taken as a measure of the long-term balance for the capital structure. Thus:

(i)   Equity provides 105/150.

(ii) Debt provides 45/150.

(c) WACC is found by the summation of weights × component costs:

$$\%$$

Equity: $\dfrac{105}{150} \times 13.3\% = \quad 9.31$

Debt: $\dfrac{35}{150} \times 8.4\% = \quad \underline{1.96}$

$$\underline{11.27}$$

In order to facilitate the use of discount tables the WACC is rounded down to 11%.

The directors are arguing about the appropriate discount rate; their arguments involve three points:

(a) *Marginal cost of capital* The marketing director's comments are inappropriate. Bank interest rate is the appropriate rate for investments in that particular risk class; the context of the question indicates property to be in a different risk class. It must also be remembered that financing decisions are not independent of future financial requirements, using relatively cheap debt now may require equity funding at a later date.

(b) *Low risk of property investments* In order to deal with this in a satisfactory manner, information relating to the type and degree of risk is necessary. Unsystematic risk can be diversified away within a portfolio, therefore one assumes it is a different systematic risk class and if beta is less than one then a lower rate of discount is appropriate.

(c) *Weighted average cost of capital* The comments of the finance director presuppose that the average risk of the firm's assets corresponds with that of property. If property risk is less then using the WACC may result in the rejection of worthwhile projects.

Usefulness and limitations of the weighted average cost of capital

The WACC is commonly used as the discount rate in the appraisal of new investment projects, despite the difficulties inherent in estimating it and the theoretical limitations in its use. Whatever the theoretical arguments, in practice a company must seek a consistent and workable basis for a target discount rate which can be routinely applied to evaluate the large number of investment decisions which must be made. WACC is commonly recognised as such a basis.

As we have already noted in calculating WACC the company must first estimate the cost of each type of capital being used. These 'costs' (expressed as a percentage), are the minimum returns which must be given to the suppliers of each type of capital to justify them supplying the capital. Each project must earn a return at least equal to the return which must be given to the supplier of capital, to be justified. Thus from a simplistic viewpoint, if a project is discounted at a 'weighted average' of the return required by each type of capital which is used to finance it, then if NPV is positive the project must be making cash returns more than sufficient to give the necessary minimum cash return to the supplier of capital.

Under certain conditions WACC can be regarded as the 'opportunity' cost of using funds. Such an opportunity cost is consistent with any economic decision-making criteria. The cost of both equity and debt will reflect the return that suppliers of capital can make by other investments in similar risk class. Any variation in cash flow pattern between that supplied by the project and that required by borrowing or lending in the capital market. This view is, however, limited by the necessary assumption of a project capital market. If such a market does not exist, then the WACC will not necessarily reflect a true opportunity cost.

The use of WACC is also limited if the company faces a situation of capital rationing whereby it cannot raise as much finance as it would like. Here WACC will again not necessarily be the opportunity cost of capital as the true opportunity cost must reflect the return on investment opportunities which cannot be undertaken because of the capital constraint.

It might be suggested that in practice a company does not finance any particular project from a 'mix' of capital sources but might issue, say, debt to finance a particular project. However, the use of WACC avoids the problems of identifying a particular source of finance. The company will regard all projects as being financed out of a 'pool' of funds which is continually being expanded from different sources. The investment and financing decision can thus be separated. However, the use of WACC is thus limited by the assumption that the company will raise finance in such a way as to keep the weighting of sources of finance constant in this pool of funds. Solomons argued in 1963 that this was justified as a company's capital structure would only change slowly over time. Thus WACC would appear to be justified as the method for estimating the cost of financing any new project provided the project is *marginal* in nature and not of such a size that its financing would alter the weightings of the capital sources and the WACC.

The most severe limitations on the use of WACC are the implicit assumptions about risk inherent in its use.

WEIGHTED MARGINAL COST OF CAPITAL

The weighted average cost of capital may vary at any time depending on the volume of financing the firm plans to raise. As the volume of financing increases, the cost of the various types of financing will increase, thereby raising the firm's weighted average cost of capital. A schedule or graph relating the firm's weighted average cost of capital to the level of new financing is called the weighted marginal cost of capital (WMCC).

In order to calculate its weighted marginal cost of capital, the firm must first determine the cost of each source of financing at various levels of total financing. To do this it must take the following steps:

(a) The cost of each source of financing for various levels of use of that type of financing must be determined by an analysis of current market conditions.

(b) The level of *total new financing* at which the cost of the new components changes must be determined. This is calculated using the historic or target capital structure proportions of debt, preferred stock, and common stock equity. The levels at which the component costs increase are called *breaking points*; they are calculated using the following formula:

$$BP_i = \frac{TF_i}{Pr_i}$$

where BP_i = breaking point for financing source 'i'
       TF_i = total new financing from source 'i' at the breaking point
       Pr_i = capital structure proportion — historic or target — for financing type 'i'

THEORY OF CAPITAL STRUCTURE

The theory of capital structure is closely related to the firm's cost of capital. The debate concerns whether or not there is an 'optimal' capital structure. Those who assert the existence of an optimal capital structure are said to take a *traditional* approach, while those who believe an optimal capital structure does not exist are referred to as supporters of the MM (Modigliani and Miller) capital structure theory.

Traditional theory of capital structure

The traditional theory of capital structure is that as the level of gearing increases within a moderate range of gearing ratios, so the average cost of capital will fall. This is because debt finance is cheaper than equity finance, and provided the proportion of debt capital remains small:

(a) There will be adequate profits to pay interest, and adequate capital to provide security, so that successive borrowings can be made without increased risk to the *lenders* and without any increase in the interest rate.

(b) There will be adequate profits to ensure a dividend after the loan interest has been paid, and no reason why lenders should need to involve themselves with the management of the company provided the conditions of their loans are fulfilled so that successive borrowings can be made without increased risk to the ordinary shareholders and consequently without any fall in the share price, i.e., without any increase in the effective cost of equity capital.

The traditional theory also holds that as gearing is increased there will come a point at which lenders feel less assured that the company will always be able to service its loan capital, and shareholders become uneasy that the business may be conducted primarily to satisfy lenders' requirements with only a residual regard for the return on equity. At that point the cost of both types of capital will begin to rise, and further gearing will in fact increase the average cost of capital employed. This is illustrated in Figure 1.

Modigliani-Miller (MM) theory of capital structure

MM maintained that if tax is ignored, the financial structure of the company will *not* affect the average cost of capital. They argue that the total market value of the organisation (and therefore its cost of capital) should be independent of the debt/equity relationship. For market value to be independent of the capital structure, the weighted average cost of capital would need to stay constant over a range of debt/equity ratios. This implies that the cost of equity rises *as soon as* debt is issued and continues to rise as further debt is issued. Hence the effective cost of debt equals the cost of equity. Figure 2 illustrates this.

Assumption of the MM analysis It must be noted that the MM analysis is based on four assumptions:

(a) A world of no taxes.
(b) No transactions costs and rational economic behaviour.
(c) Individuals can borrow at the same rate of interest as commercial organisations.
(d) Organisations in equivalent risk categories can be identified.

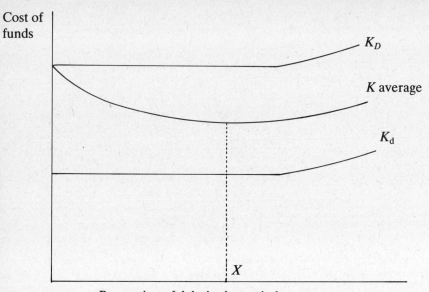

Figure 1   Optimal capital structure — traditional view

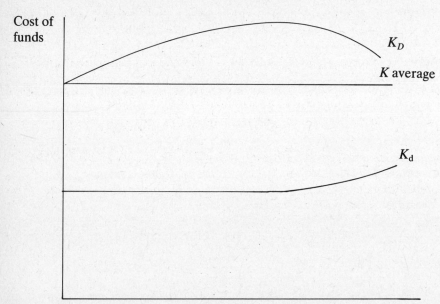

Figure 2   Optimal capital structure — the MM view

7   Capital expenditure decisions

The point of capital budgeting — indeed, the point of all financial analysis — is to make decisions that will maximise the value of the firm's share capital. The capital budgeting process is designed to answer two questions:

(a) Which of several mutually exclusive investments should be selected?
(b) How many projects, in total, should be accepted?

The principal methods of evaluating capital projects are:

(a) the return on investment method;
(b) the pay-back method;
(c) discounted cash flow (DCF):
   (i)   the net present value method (NPV);
   (ii) the internal rate of return method (IRR).

NPV is the present value of future returns discounted at the appropriate cost of capital, minus the cost of investment. IRR is the interest rate which equates the present value of future returns to the investment outlay.

RETURN ON INVESTMENT METHOD

A capital investment project may be assessed by calculating the return on investment, or accounting rate of return, and comparing it with a predetermined target level. There are several different definitions of 'return on investment', the most popular being:

$$\text{ARR} = \frac{\text{Estimated average profits}}{\text{Estimated average investment}} \times 100\%$$

Example 1   Ragwort Ltd is considering buying a new combine harvester to add to its fleet. It has two alternatives:

	Combine A	Combine B
	£	£
Cost	60,000	60,000
Estimated residual value	10,000	10,000
Estimated life	10 years	10 years
Estimated future profits		
(before depreciation): Year 1	15,000	10,000
2	15,000	10,500
3	13,000	12,500
4	11,500	13,000
5	11,500	15,000
6	9,000	15,000
7	8,000	17,000
8	8,000	17,500
9	6,000	18,500
10	5,000	18,000

We can use ARR to assess which alternative should be chosen, as follows:

	A (£)	B (£)
Total profits before depreciation	102,000	142,000
Total depreciation	10,000	11,000
Total profits after depreciation	92,000	131,000
Average profits (10 years)	9,200	13,100
Value of investment at beginning	60,000	60,000
Value of investment at end	10,000	11,000

Average value of investment: ARR:

A: $\dfrac{60,000 + 10,000}{2} = £35,000$ $\dfrac{9,200}{35,000} \times 100 = 26\%$

B: $\dfrac{60,000 + 11,000}{2} = £35,500$ $\dfrac{13,100}{35,500} \times 100 = 37\%$

Using the ARR as a criterion for project selection, combine B should be purchased as it yields the greater return investment.

The return on investment is a measure of profitability and its major advantages are that it can be obtained from readily available accounting data and that its meaning is widely understood. Its major shortcomings are that it is based on accounting profits rather than cash flows and that it fails to take account of the timing of cash inflows and outflows.

PAY-BACK METHOD

Pay-back periods are commonly used to evaluate proposed investments. The method has two major uses. First, it can be used to help make, accept or reject decisions. The decision rule in this case would depend upon whether the time that it would take to pay back the cost of investment would be acceptable. To improve this decision rule, it can be made more sophisticated by the introduction of a *finite horizon*, which means that management will only accept investment opportunities to their organisation which have a pay-back period of less than the *n* years of the finite horizon.

The second use of the pay-back method is in ranking decisions. The decision rule in this case will be to give preference to those investment projects with the shortest pay-back periods.

The pay-back period is a better measure than the average rate of return since it considers cash flows rather than accounting profits. Only cash inflows can pay the firm's bills. The pay-back period is also a superior measure in that it gives some implicit consideration to the timing of cash flows and therefore the time factor of the value of money. A final reason why many firms use the payback period as a decision criterion, or as a supplement to sophisticated decision criteria, is that it is a measure of risk. The pay-back period reflects the liquidity of a project and thereby the risk of recovering the investment. The more liquid an investment is, the less risky it is assumed to be, and vice versa .

Example 2 Two projects are being considered by a firm; each requires an investment of £1,000. The firm's marginal cost of capital is 10%. The net cash flows from investment A and B are shown in the following table:

	Net cash flows	
	A	B
Year	£	£
1	500	100
2	400	200
3	300	300
4	100	400
5		500
6		600

The pay-back period is the number of years it takes a firm to recover its original investment from net cash flows. Since the cost is £1,000, the pay-back period is 2⅓ years for project A and 4 years for project B. If the firm were employing a 3-year pay-back period, project A would be accepted but project B would be rejected.

The pay-back period method has a number of disadvantages, which are evident in this example. It ignores income beyond the pay-back period (i.e., when a finite horizon is imposed on the analysis). If the project is one maturing in later years, the use of the pay-back period can lead to the selection of less desirable investments. Projects with longer pay-back periods are characteristically those involved in long-range planning — developing a new product or market. These are strategic decisions which determine a firm's fundamental position, but they also involve investments which do not yield their highest returns for a number of years. This means that the pay-back method may be biased against the very investments that are most important to a firm's long-run success.

Recognition of the longer period over which an investment is likely to yield savings points to a weakness in the use of the pay-back method for ranking investment proposals: its failure to take into account the time value of money. This can be seen in example 3.

Example 3   Consider two assets, X and Y, each costing £300 and each having the following cash flows:

Year	X £	Y £
1	200	100
2	100	200
3	100	100

Each project has a two-year pay-back; hence, each would appear equally desirable. However, we know that a pound today is worth more than a pound next year, so project X, with its faster cash flow, is certainly more desirable.

Perhaps this method can only be justified if:

(a) There is the possibility of a high degree of obsolescence applying to some aspect of the investment opportunity under consideration.

(b) Where there may be some other risks attached to the opportunities being considered, for example, where an investment is made in a foreign country which has political instability so the cost of investment needs to be recovered as soon as possible.

COMPOUNDING AND DISCOUNTING

The principle underlying compounding concerns the fact that any sum will 'grow' if loaned out in return for interest being added to it. Discounting, on the other hand, concerns the concept that any sum of money which is to be received at some time in the future will 'shrink' to less than that of the expected future sum.

Compounding: $S = P(1 + r)^n$

where S = sum to be received in the future

P = present value of the investment

r = rate of interest expressed as a proportion

n = number of years' time at the end of which the sum S will be received

Discounting: $P = \dfrac{S}{(1 + r)^n}$ or $S \times \dfrac{1}{(1 + r)^n}$

The rather tedious method of discounting future values by means of the formula can be overcome by means of discount tables. These tables show the present value of £1 receivable at varying intervals of time and for a wide range of interest rates.

NET PRESENT VALUE METHOD

Flaws in the pay-back method led to the development of discounted cash flow (DCF) techniques to take account of the time value of money. One such discounted cash flow technique is the net present value method. The calculation of NPV is one of the most commonly used sophisticated capital budgeting techniques. The definition of NPV is:

NPV = Present value of cash flows − Initial investment

It is found by subtracting the initial investment in a project from the present value of the cash inflows discounted at a rate equal to the firm's cost of capital. If the net present value is positive, the project should be accepted; if negative, it should be rejected. If the two projects are mutually exclusive, the one with the higher NPV should be chosen.

Example 4   G. Trotter, a precocious schoolboy, has £20 which he decides to invest if he can be reasonably confident that his investment will earn at least 10% per annum. He is considering three projects, each of which would cost £20 to begin:

(a) Project A would earn £21.80 (9%) at the end of the first year.

(b) Project B would earn £25.00 (25%) at the end of the first year.

(c) Project C would earn £14 at the end of the first year and £10 at the end of the second year.

If none of these projects is undertaken G. Trotter will invest his £20 in something else which will earn 10% per year.

G. Trotter expects to earn 10% per annum with his investment of £20; thus he would want £22 if the project ended at the end of year 1. Project A which ends in year 1 is expected to return only £21.80, therefore it would not earn 10% per annum and is unsatisfactory.

In order to earn 10% per annum G. Trotter would require £22 back at the end of the first year; £22 is no more and no less than is expected from his £20. In other words, £22 in year one is only just as good as £20 now, because the £20 now will earn an extra £2 in the course of the year (ignoring inflation).

To convert from future values to present values we are simply discounting: £20 in year 0 should pay back £22 at the end of year 1 (20 × 1.10 is compounding); therefore £22 in year 1 is the same value as £22 × 1/1.10 = £22 × 0.9091 = £20 in year 0 (discounting).

Project A would be expected to earn £21.80 at the end of year 1 which is less than the required 10% per annum. In other words, if money invested earns 10%, less than £20 should be required in order to pay back £21.80 in year 1:

£21.80 in year 1 is the same value as £21.80 × 1/1.10
= £21.80 × 0.9091
= £19.81 in year 0 (now).

The present value of £21.80 in year 1, given that money invested earns 10% per annum is £19.81. As project A requires an initial outlay of £20 we have:

	£
Present value of income from project A	19.81
Present value of cost of project A	20.00
Net present value	(0.19)

The negative net present value indicates that the project would fail to make the expected return (in this case 10% per annum).

Project B is expected to earn £25 at the end of year 2, which is more than the required 10% per annum. In other words, if money earned is exactly 10% per annum, the investment needed to pay back £25 in year 2 would be more than £20:

£25 in year 2 is the same value as £25 × 1/(1.10)^2
= £25 × 0.8264
= £20.66 in year 0.

The present value of £25 in year 2, given that money earns 10% per annum, is £20.66. As project B requires an outlay of £20, we have:

	£
Present value of income from project B	20.66
Present value of cost of project B	20.00
	0.66
Net present value	

The positive net present value indicates that the project would earn at more than the required rate of return.

The same approach may be applied to project C:

	£
The present value of cost is	(20.00)
Income:	
The present value of £14 in year 1 is:	
$14 \times 1/1.10 =$	12.72
The present value of £10 in year 2 is:	
$10 \times 1/(1.10)^2 =$	8.26
Net present value	0.98

The positive net present value indicates that the project would earn cash at more than the required rate of 10% per annum.

Project B has a net present value of 66p and project C one of 98p. All other things being equal, project C should therefore be undertaken in preference to project B. Although the total return from project B, £25, is greater than the total return from project C, £24, the timing of the returns, i.e., the £14 earned in year 1 by project C, should influence the decision in favour of project C.

Example 5 A farmer is considering installing grain drying equipment to handle 1,400 tonnes of winter wheat. The cost of this is £56,000. Two other factors need to be considered:

(a) Grain drying equipment: Productive life = 12 years
                              Running costs   = £6 per tonne
(b) Grain drying by contractor   = £11 per tonne

If we assume that the rate of inflation is zero, then the grain drying equipment will yield an income of £5 per tonne for 12 years, i.e., £7,000 on the assumption of an average harvest.

The farmer, in deciding whether to purchase, must compare the present value of £7,000 per year each year for 12 years with the current cost of £56,000 of purchasing the grain dryer. If the present value (NPV) is greater than the price of the grain dryer, he will invest.

NPV   = Discounted sum of future incomes generated by an investment
               project
£56,000   = Asset price
£7,000   = Rental price

To compare NPV with asset price we need a rate of interest — assume this to be 10%

Current value of £7,000 in 1 year's time = $7,000/(1 + r) = 7,000/1.1$.

Current value of £7,000 in 2 years' time = $7,000/(1 + r)^2 = 7,000/1.21$.

$$\text{NPV} = \frac{7,000}{(1+r)} + \frac{7,000}{(1+r)^2} + \frac{7,000}{(1+r)^3} \cdots \frac{7,000}{(1+r)^{11}} + \frac{7,000}{(1+r)^{12}}$$
$$= 6,363 + 5,782 + 5,259 \ldots \ldots \ldots + 2,450 + 3,233$$
$$= 47,698$$
$$\text{NPV} = 47,698, \text{ the asset price} = £56,000.$$

Therefore the farmer will not invest since NPV is less than asset price.

If the rate of interest falls to 5%, then NPV = £62,041, NPV is greater than the asset price, and therefore the farmer will invest.

Example 6 The management of C. Fret Ltd is considering the purchase of a new machine at a cost of £10,000. It would last for four years and have a residual value of £3,600. Annual running costs would be £8,000 and use of the machine would increase revenue by £11,000 per annum. The company's cost of capital is 12%. Ignoring taxation and inflation, the management must evaluate the project.

The residual value of the machine is assumed to be received as cash at the beginning of year 5, i.e., in year 4.

Year	Net cash flow £	Discount factor	Present value of cash flow £	Cumulative PV £
0	(10,000)	1	(10,000)	(10,000)
1	3,000	1/1.12	2,678	(7,322)
2	3,000	$1/(1.12)^2$	2,391	(4,931)
3	3,000	$1/(1.12)^3$	2,135	(2,796)
4	3,000	$1/(1.12)^4$	1,906	(890)
4	3,600	$1/(1.12)^4$	2,288	1,398

NPV = £1,398.

The NPV is the difference between the present value of benefits, £11,398, and the present value of costs, £10,000. In this example the NPV is positive, which means that the project would earn more than the required 12%.

Annuity approach

Using the annuity approach all investment opportunities are discounted back to their NPVs. These NPVs are then converted into an annual figure for the stream of earnings which run over the period of the particular project's life. The values of the annual figures for the stream of each project's earnings can then be compared.

Ranking projects

When projects need to be ranked for approval purposes their NPVs in absolute terms rarely provide a good indication of which is the most appropriate to be undertaken simply through the order of these rankings. For the amount of the initial outlay in absolute terms must also be brought into the analysis. For example, from the following data it can be seen that project X has the highest NPV:

Projects	Capital outlay	Present value	NPV
X	300	340	40
Y	200	230	30
Z	100	125	25

However, the question needs to be asked as to whether this comparison of NPVs in absolute terms is really meaningful. The answer must be no, as it is the NPV per unit of investment which is important. This can be ascertained in the form of a profitability (or cost benefit) ratio, from:

$$\frac{\text{PV of future benefits}}{\text{PV of future costs}}$$

The profitability ratios of the projects in the above table can now be calculated as follows:

PV/Capital outlay = Profitability ratio

X	340/300 = 1.13
Y	230/200 = 1.15
Z	125/100 = 1.25

As project Z has the highest profitability ratio this would be the most beneficial one to carry out. Therefore, if an organisation has £300 to invest and three of project Z could be undertaken it would be better for them to do this rather than to carry out one of project X. However, if for some reason only one of each project could be undertaken it would be better to consider the NPVs of these in absolute terms. Note that this assumes the problem of capital rationing is for a single period.

INTERNAL RATE OF RETURN

The IRR is probably the most used technique for evaluating investment alternatives, but is considerably more difficult to calculate than NPV. IRR is defined as 'the rate of discount that equates the present value of cash inflows with the initial investment associated with a project'. The IRR, in other words, is the discount rate which equates the NPV of an investment opportunity with zero.

$$\frac{F_1}{1+r} + \frac{F_2}{(1+r)^2} + \ldots + \frac{F_n}{(1+r)^n} - I = 0$$

where F = Cash flow, I = Initial investment, r = IRR

We do not know the value of r. Thus we have an equation with one unknown, and we can solve for the value of r. Some value of r will cause the sum of the discounted receipts to equal the initial cost of the project making the equation equal to nil — the solution value of r is therefore the IRR.

Example 7   Returning to example 5 (the farmer investing in a £56,000 grain dryer) we can calculate the IRR as follows:

Select r such that NPV = 0

$$56,000 = \frac{7,000}{1+r} + \frac{7,000}{(1+r)^2} + \ldots + \frac{7,000}{(1+r)^{12}}$$

$r \approx 6.9\%$

This indicates that money invested in the grain dryer is given a return that is approximately equal to 6.9% per annum.

Example 8   If £400 is invested today and generates £500 in one year's time the internal rate of return (r) can be calculated as follows:

PV of cost = PV of benefits
400 = 500/(1 + r)   (PV of 500 in one year's time)
1 + r = 500/400
1 + r = 1.25
r = 0.25, or 25%

Example 9 Senator Terry Trufo's firm, TT Bonus Inc, has undertaken some legal and academic research, at a cost of £4,000, into the possibilities of selling university degrees. The firm is unsure of the outcome of such a venture but feel that there is a 60% chance of annual income of £70,000 and a 40% chance of annual income of £40,000.

Printing machinery would need to be bought at a cost of some £40,000 payable in two equal annual instalments, one immediately and one in one year's time if the equipment had been operating correctly for a year. The equipment would be depreciated on a straight-line basis by £3,500 per annum for 10 years and then sold. Use would also be made of some existing equipment which: originally cost £6,000; has a book value of £1,000; would cost £9,000 to replace, although the firm is considering selling it for £2,000.

Production and labour costs in the first year would amount to £55,000 payable in one year's time, although the next nine years' costs would fall to £30,000 if demand was low in the first year. Revenue would first be receivable in two years' time and for the following nine years. Fixed costs of £5,000 p.a. would be reallocated to the degree project.

The IRR can be calculated as follows:

Year		Cash flows	Present value at	
			8%	10%
		£000	£	£
0	Existing equipment	(2)	(2,000)	(2,000)
0	Machinery	(20)	(20,000)	(20,000)
1	Machinery	(20)	(18,519)	(18,182)
1	Costs	(55)	(50,926)	(50,000)
2-10	Costs	(45)	(260,287)	(235,600)
2-11	Revenue	58	360,357	323,986
10	Sale proceeds	5	2,316	1,928
			10,941	132

Internal rate of return = 8% + (10,941/(10,941 − 132)) × 2% = 10% (to the nearest 0.1%)

Arguments in favour of the IRR method

Two arguments in favour of the IRR method are:

(a) Most businessmen can readily understand the concept of a rate of return, but not the meaning of an NPV. It is likely, however, that a discounted rate of return would be easily confused with an accounting rate of return, and it is necessary for businessmen to learn about NPV and understand what it means.

(b) The IRR indicates the margin of error in an investment decision, given the uncertainty which is inevitably present in all estimates. This argument is only partly true, however, since the IRR is an indication of the sensitivity of a project to the size of the discount rate; it is not a useful indicator of the sensitivity of a project to wrong estimates of cash flows.

COMPARISON OF NPV AND IRR

The key difference between the NPV and IRR approaches is that the NPV approach assumes that all intermediate cash flows are reinvested at the firm's cost of capital, whereas the IRR approach assumes reinvestment at the IRR.

Different ranking of projects under NPV and IRR

Although the NPV and IRR methods will always give an identical 'accept or reject' decision they will often rank projects in a different order (assuming that ranking is based upon the absolute size of the net present value in the NPV method and by the size of the yield in the case of IRR method). Example 10 will help to show why this is so.

Example 10

Year	Cash flow Project A £	Cash flow Project B £
0	−100	−100
1	30	—
2	130	169

Both projects earn a 30% return on investment. Project A withdraws its yield at the end of year 1 (£30) while project B reinvests this at 30% to earn a further £9 during the second year.

The IRR method would show both projects as equally desirable. However, providing the cost of capital was less than 30%, the NPV method would rank project B higher.

These differences in the ranking order arise because of the different assumptions which the two techniques make regarding the rate at which cash flows received during the life of the project may be reinvested. The NPV method assumes that such flows may be reinvested to earn a rate equivalent to the company's cost of capital, while the IRR method assumes reinvestment to earn a yield equal to that on the entire project.

In example 10 therefore, the IRR's conclusion is only correct if the withdrawal of £30 from project A at the end of year 1 can be reinvested in another venture yielding 30%.

Conflicting results

One method of determining which is the superior project when differing results have been obtained from the use of NPV and IRR techniques is the incremental yield approach.

Example 11 Two projects with the same lives but differing initial capital outlays

Project	Capital cost (£000)	Life (years)	Annual cash flow (£000)	NPV at 8% (£000)	IRR
A	502	10	100	169	15%
B	780	10	144	186	13%

To arrive at the incremental yield, the cash flow of the project with the smaller capital investment is subtracted from that of the higher. The internal rate of return is then calculated on the resultant net flows:

Project	Capital cost (£000)	Life (years)	Annual cash flow (£000)	NPV at 8% (£000)	Incremental yield IRR
B – A	278	10	44	17	9.4%

The resultant incremental yield (9.4%) is then compared with the company's cost of capital (8%). If it exceeds this cost by an adequate margin (depending on the degree of risk involved in the assurance of the returns) then the project with the larger initial capital outlay should be chosen (in this example project B), since it provides all that the alternative project can, and in addition, a positive and significant return on the incremental investment.

It should be remembered, however, that if the incremental cash flows are at a higher degree of risk, thus requiring a return in excess of 9.4%, then project A is to be preferred.

Although example 11 compares two projects with the same lives but differing initial capital outlays, the incremental yield technique is also suitable for comparing projects that have different lives and/or different capital outlays.

Arguments for and against the two methods

In the past a number of opinions have been put forward arguing the case for and against both methods.

H. Bierman and S. Smidt *The Capital Budgeting Decision* 5th ed, Macmillan, 1980 suggest that the NPV technique is preferable to the IRR technique for the following three reasons:

(a) Because the IRR method reflects the average rather than the incremental cash flows it may offer an incorrect recommendation when mutually exclusive projects are under consideration. This they term as the 'scale' and 'size' problem. Because the IRR is a percentage and not an absolute value, a 20% return on £100 appears more attractive than a 19% return on £100,000.

(b) In order to determine which of a pair of IRR mutually exclusive projects is superior, the internal rates of return of the incremental cash proceeds need to be computed. If there are only two such mutually exclusive projects under review by a firm this procedure is not unduly burdensome. If, however, there are, say, 51 projects being considered there would need to be 50 computations, since 50 projects would need to be eliminated. The NPV method does not present this difficulty.

(c) The third disadvantage pointed out by Bierman and Smidt is that it is possible for a project to have more than one IRR. It is therefore understandably confusing to management if they are informed that a project has two returns, one of 4% and one of 24%. To see how this is possible, consider the cash flows for the investment below:

Year	Cash flow
0	−1,000
1	3,100
2	−2,200

The IRR for this investment is both 10% and 100%, and although this problem can be overcome by further analysis, it nevertheless is an unnecessary added complication.

Bierman and Smidt did not accept that because the NPV method required a minimum acceptable discount rate to be agree upon before the technique could be utilised, this therefore made it inferior to the IRR method. They acknowledged that it was indeed a problem, but that it was one that had to be similarly faced with the IRR procedure, since this required a minimum acceptable discount rate to be compared with the IRR value before a decision could be made.

A. J. Merrett and A. Sykes, *The Finance and Analysis of Capital Projects* 2nd ed, Longman, 1973, however, 'strongly preferred' the IRR method, for three reasons also:

(a) It is, they believe, a more useful measure of profitability when endeavouring to assess the return offered for bearing risk. They maintain that a main characteristic of the type of risk normally encountered in business is related to time (which generally increases through time). Because this time factor is in turn related to the amount of capital outstanding in a project at any given period, and because the figure provided by the discounted IRR method is the rate of return per unit of time, then it is therefore essentially measuring return in the same dimensions (time and quantity) as risk. This in their opinion facilitates the task of determining whether the return offered is adequate given the risks involved. They feel that NPV, being an absolute quantity, lacks this important advantage.

(b) From their own experience they found that the IRR technique was more easily understood and accepted by businessmen, since they tended to think more in terms of a rate of return on capital than 'present values of future cash flows'.

(c) Merrett and Sykes' third point again brings up the argument that the IRR technique is not subject to the dispute concerning the determination of a figure to represent the firm's cost of capital. However, their emphasis is placed on the contention that as it is so difficult to arrive at one figure that will represent this cost, in a real world situation a list of present values would be calculated using different discounting factors. Thus when the NPV technique is used and the results given to management, the presentation is large and cumbersome. The end-product, therefore, is more likely to confuse than enlighten. This problem, they felt, was not necessary and could be avoided if a single figure was offered. This the IRR method makes possible.

R. J. Briston and J. Liversidge *A Practical Approach to Business Investment Decisions*, Macmillan, 1979, sum the question up as follows: 'On balance the IRR method tends to be more popular in practice, while the NPV method is advocated by most academics.'

Table 1 Cumulative present value factors: The table gives the present value of 'n' annual payments of £1 received for the next 'n' years with a constant discount of x% per year. (For example, with a discount rate of 7% and with 6 annual payments of £1 the present value is £4.767.)

Years 0 to:	1%	2%	3%	4%	5%	6%	7%	8%	9%	10%
1	0.990	0.980	0.971	0.962	0.952	0.943	0.935	0.926	0.917	0.909
2	1.970	1.942	1.913	1.886	1.859	1.833	1.808	1.783	1.759	1.736
3	2.941	2.884	2.829	2.775	2.723	2.673	2.624	2.577	2.531	2.487
4	3.902	3.808	3.717	3.630	3.546	3.465	3.387	3.312	3.240	3.170
5	4.853	4.713	4.580	4.452	4.329	4.212	4.100	3.993	3.890	3.791
6	5.795	5.601	5.417	5.242	5.076	4.917	4.767	4.623	4.486	4.355
7	6.728	6.472	6.230	6.002	5.786	5.582	5.389	5.206	5.033	4.868
8	7.652	7.325	7.020	6.733	6.463	6.210	5.971	5.747	5.535	5.335
9	8.566	8.162	7.786	7.435	7.108	6.802	6.515	6.247	5.995	5.759
10	9.471	8.983	8.530	8.111	7.722	7.360	7.024	6.710	6.418	6.145
11	10.368	9.787	9.253	8.760	8.306	7.887	7.499	7.139	6.805	6.495
12	11.255	10.575	9.954	9.385	8.863	8.384	7.943	7.536	7.161	6.814
13	12.134	11.348	10.635	9.986	9.394	8.853	8.358	7.904	7.487	7.103
14	13.004	12.106	11.296	10.563	9.899	9.295	8.745	8.244	7.786	7.367
15	13.865	12.849	11.938	11.118	10.380	9.712	9.108	8.559	8.061	7.606
16	14.718	13.578	12.561	11.652	10.838	10.106	9.447	8.851	8.313	7.824
17	15.562	14.292	13.166	12.166	11.274	10.477	9.763	9.122	8.544	8.022
18	16.398	14.922	13.754	12.659	11.690	10.828	10.059	9.372	8.756	8.201
19	17.226	15.678	14.324	13.134	12.085	11.158	10.336	9.604	8.950	8.365
20	18.046	16.351	14.877	13.590	12.462	11.470	10.594	9.818	9.129	8.514

Years 0 to:	11%	12%	13%	14%	15%	16%	17%	18%	19%	20%
1	0.901	0.893	0.885	0.877	0.870	0.862	0.855	0.847	0.840	0.833
2	1.713	1.690	1.668	1.647	1.626	1.605	1.585	1.566	1.547	1.528
3	2.444	2.402	2.361	2.322	2.283	2.246	2.210	2.174	2.140	2.106
4	3.102	3.037	2.974	2.914	2.855	2.798	2.743	2.690	2.639	2.589
5	3.696	3.605	3.517	3.433	3.352	3.274	3.199	3.127	3.058	2.991
6	4.231	4.111	3.998	3.889	3.784	3.685	3.589	3.498	3.410	3.326
7	4.712	4.564	4.423	4.288	4.160	4.039	3.922	3.812	3.706	3.605
8	5.146	4.968	4.799	4.639	4.487	4.344	4.207	4.078	3.954	3.837
9	5.537	5.328	5.132	4.946	4.772	4.607	4.451	4.303	4.163	4.031
10	5.889	5.650	5.426	5.216	5.019	4.833	4.659	4.494	4.339	4.192
11	6.207	5.938	5.687	5.453	5.234	5.029	4.836	4.656	4.486	4.327
12	6.492	6.194	5.918	5.660	5.421	5.197	4.988	4.793	4.611	4.439
13	6.750	6.424	6.122	5.842	5.583	5.342	5.118	4.910	4.715	4.533
14	6.982	6.628	6.302	6.002	5.724	5.468	5.229	5.008	4.802	4.611
15	7.191	6.811	6.462	6.142	5.847	5.575	5.324	5.092	4.876	4.675
16	7.379	6.974	6.604	6.265	5.954	5.668	5.405	5.162	4.938	4.730
17	7.549	7.120	6,729	6.373	6.047	5.749	5.475	5.222	4.990	4.775
18	7.702	7.250	6.840	6.467	6.128	5.818	5.534	5.273	5.033	4.812
19	7.839	7.366	6.938	6.550	6.198	5.877	5.584	5.316	5.070	4.843
20	7.963	7.469	7.025	6.623	6.259	5.929	5.628	5.353	5.101	4.870

8 Cash flows and asset replacement decisions

CASH FLOWS AND THE TIME VALUE OF MONEY

When an investment decision is made the choice is generally from a number of different opportunities which are open to management at that time. One of the major problems facing the decision-makers is the fact that invariably the sums which would have to be spent on the investment opportunities being contemplated; the capital outlay, and the cash flows which are expected to come in from them would differ both as far as the amounts and their timing are concerned.

Example 1 assume that an organisation is considering four alternative feasible investment opportunities and finds that the cash flows expected to be associated with these are as follow:

Alternative opportunity	Cash outlay t_0 £	Cash inflows t_1 £	t_2 £	t_3 £	$t4$ £	Total £
A	42	0	0	20	29	49
B	30	5	10	20	15	50
C	30	5	20	20	5	50
D	30	15	20	10	5	50

A is obviously the least favourable of the investment opportunities. As far as B, C and D are concerned, the choice between them is not so obvious because they all have exactly the same total cash outflows and inflows associated with them. Nevertheless, as the same amount is invested in all of the projects B, C and D, the project which produces its cash inflows at the earliest time would instinctively be the most favoured. The earning profiles of B, C and D are illustrated in Figure 1.

Showing cash flows diagrammatically helps to emphasise the fact that the value of money received at different time periods, even when price levels are constant, will be different. Furthermore, if the cash which is received the earliest can be re-invested this should make it obvious that B would be

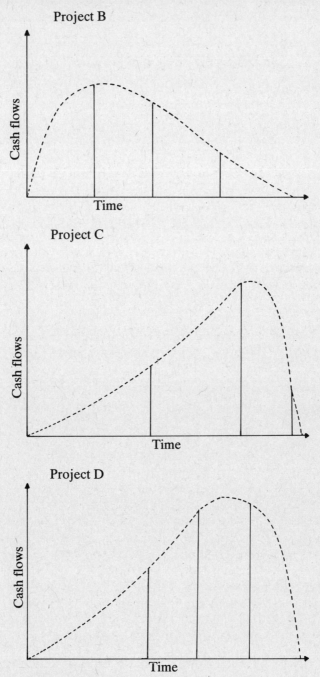

Figure 1   Earning profiles

preferred. This all means that money has a time dimension which is referred to as the *time value* of money.

The adjustment of the cash flows of a number of time periods so that their time values are brought to those of a single time period is done by either compounding or discounting them. The objective of compounding or discounting is to bring all the cash flows concerned into the terms of their 'value' at a stated time period. Discounting brings back the cash flows to be received in the future by 'shrinking' them into terms of a smaller value at the present time, whereas compounding takes them forward to a specific date in the future and in the process the addition of interest causes them to 'grow'.

The concept of cash flow is of vital importance to capital investment appraisal since the real cost to a business of any new investment project is the actual net amount of cash that flows out of the business as a result of the investment decision, and the return to the business on that project will be the actual amount of cash available to the rest of the business from the project during its life.

Discounted cash flow (DCF) is a technique of investment appraisal which is based on the concept of the 'time value of money', i.e., that £1 now has more value than £1 in the future. Future cash flows are accordingly discounted to present value equivalent amounts.

Various reasons could be suggested as to why a present £1 is worth more than a future £1:

(a) Uncertainty: the business world is full of risk and uncertainty, although there might be the promise of money to come in the future, it can never be certain that the money will be received until it has actually been paid.

(b) Inflation: due to inflation it is common sense that £1 now is worth more than £1 in the future. It is important, however, that the problem of inflation should not confuse the concept of DCF.

(c) An individual attaches more weight to current pleasures than to future ones, and would rather have £1 to spend now than £1 in a year's time. One reason suggested to justify the use of discounted cash flow techniques is this 'subjective time preference' of individuals who have the choice of consuming or investing their wealth. It has been argued that the return from investments must therefore be sufficient to persuade individuals to prefer to invest now, with the promise of future revenue, rather than to spend what they have now. Discounting is a measure of this time preference.

(d) Money is invested now to make profit in the future. DCF can be used to measure either:
    (i)   what alternative uses of money would earn (NPV method); or
    (ii) what the money is expected to earn (IRR method).

DECISION-MAKING IN CONDITIONS OF RISK AND UNCERTAINTY

So far in this chapter it has been assumed that the investment decision is made in a world where the future outcomes of projects are known with certainty. Under these conditions single value forecasts only are required by the decision-maker since by definition these will be achieved. However, in practice such conditions rarely, if ever, exist. A more realistic environment would be one where the decision-maker is confronted with projects involving different degrees of uncertainty and consequently different degrees of risk. Here a range of possible outcomes would ideally be required to reflect this. The remainder of this chapter therefore offers a number of approaches that can be used to achieve this, and which hopefully result in the ultimate investment decision being made on as knowledgeable and rational a basis as possible.

It is important at this stage to differentiate between risk and uncertainty since the terms are often used (incorrectly) synonymously. Risk refers to a situation where a project has a number of possible alternative outcomes but the probability of each occurring is known. In a situation of uncertainty, however, these probabilities are considered to be either partially or completely unknown.

All the methods of dealing with risk and uncertainty rely on developing subjective probability distribution forecasts of likely outcomes, and it must therefore be remembered that the result of whichever approach is adopted will only be as good and as representative as the probabilities that have been assigned to these outcomes. If an enterprise is to achieve a higher than average degree of success in picking out profitable projects for investment, its whole forecasting system must be of the highest standard. It is for this reason that the importance of developing accurate subjective probabilities cannot be overemphasised.

Risk-adjusted discount rate

This method of taking uncertainty into account is based on the rationale that a risky project will not be accepted unless it offers a premium over and above that which can be provided by a risk-free project (i.e., the risk-free rate of return). Furthermore, the more uncertain the expected future returns, the greater the risk and the greater the premium required.

Clarke, Hindelang and Pritchard, *Capital Budgeting, Planning and Control of Capital Expenditures,* Prentice Hall, 1979, suggest that the risk-adjusted rate is representable by the following equation:

$$r' = i + u + a$$

where r' = risk-adjusted discount rate
        i = risk-free rate
        u = adjustment for the firm's normal risk
        a = adjustment for above (or below) the firm's normal risk

(Note that $i + u$ is equal to the firm's cost of capital because that is the discount rate which is appropriate for projects having 'average' or 'normal' risk.)

Instead of altering the discount rate for each project it might be more convenient to place each investment in a category which will represent the risk it involves. An appropriate discount rate could then be allocated to each category, e.g.:

Category	Discount rate (%)
Very low risk (refunding a bond issue)	6
Low risk (replacement of essential machinery)	10
Average risk (normal projects)	14
High risk (new market for existing product)	18
Very high risk (research and development)	25

Obviously with both methods the actual risk-adjusted discount rates used will depend on management's perception of the risks involved and their willingness to accept risk.

Although very widely used in practice, adjusting the discount rate as a means of incorporating uncertainty into the investment decision has a number of severe limitations. Firstly, it again treats risk as a function of time by the relatively heavier discounting that it applies to the more distant cash flows. In Table 1 the organisation's cost of capital is 12% but to allow for risk a discount factor of 18% is applied.

Table 1   Effect of time on the risk-adjusted discount rate

Years	1	2	3	4	5	6
Project's cash inflows (£000)	2,000	2,000	2,000	2,000	2,000	2,000
NPV @ 12%	1,786	1,594	1,424	1,272	1,134	1,014
NPV @ 18%	1,654	1,436	1,218	1,032	874	740
Reduction due to percentage increase in discount factor (%)	7	10	14	19	23	27

The above example illustrates the effect time has on the later periods of a project's life in terms of its cash flows. This percentage reduction increases at an exponential rate because of the compounding process associated with the discount factors.

Another inadequacy of this method is that by applying a constant risk-adjusted discount rate, it is inherently assumed that all the cash flows have identical risks ascribed to them. This may be inappropriate for estimates relating to certain projects. For example, consider the life cycle of a typical product: introduction, growth, maturity and decline. For most products the first two stages, introduction and growth, will be subject to the greatest uncertainty, with the latter two being relatively easy to predict since at this stage competition is often the only variable likely to complicate the issue. A discount rate which is initially high but reducing throughout the life of the project, would therefore be far more suitable in these situations than one which remains constant and thus takes no account of the timeliness of the risks involved.

A third criticism is put forward by Louderback and Manners in 'Evaluating risky investment projects', *American Management Accounting*, February 1979, who argue that this method assumes that all the future net cash inflows can be re-invested at the adjusted discount factor. This they believe to be an incorrect assumption when the risk-adjusted discount factor is above the firm's cost of capital, since in their opinion the bulk of a firm's capital is likely to be invested at somewhere close to this cost of capital. If this is so, it is therefore inappropriate and practically unsound to expect a high risk project to produce the desired return rate when its cash inflows are unlikely to be re-invested at the adjusted discount rate.

Because of the limitations set out above and as there appears to be no satisfactory theoretical foundation for the construction in practice of either the appropriate premium rate or the different categories, other than on a purely subjective basis, this method is therefore considered relatively crude compared to some of the more sophisticated techniques that are available.

Use of simulation in the appraisal process

Simulation is the imitation of a real-world system by using a mathematical model which captures the critical operating characteristics of the system as it moves through time encountering random events. Clarke, Hindelang and Pritchard (1979).

Sensitivity analysis This is a crude but simple form of simulation. The objective is obtained by changing the values of the estimates of the key variables to determine the degree of variance that will result in the decision criterion. This will then identify which variables are the most sensitive and therefore which variables must be estimated most accurately.

Example 2   Identification of critical variables using sensitivity analysis

Key variable:	Original NPV (£)	Revised NPV (£)	Increase (Decrease) (£)	Change %
Sales price				
20% increase	100,000	150,000	50,000	50
20% decrease	100,000	60,000	(40,000)	40
Sales volume				
20% increase	100,000	180,000	80,000	80
20% decrease	100,000	0	(100,000)	100
Residual value				
20% increase	100,000	105,000	5,000	5
20% decrease	100,000	95,000	(5,000)	5

This can be represented graphically, as in Figure 2.

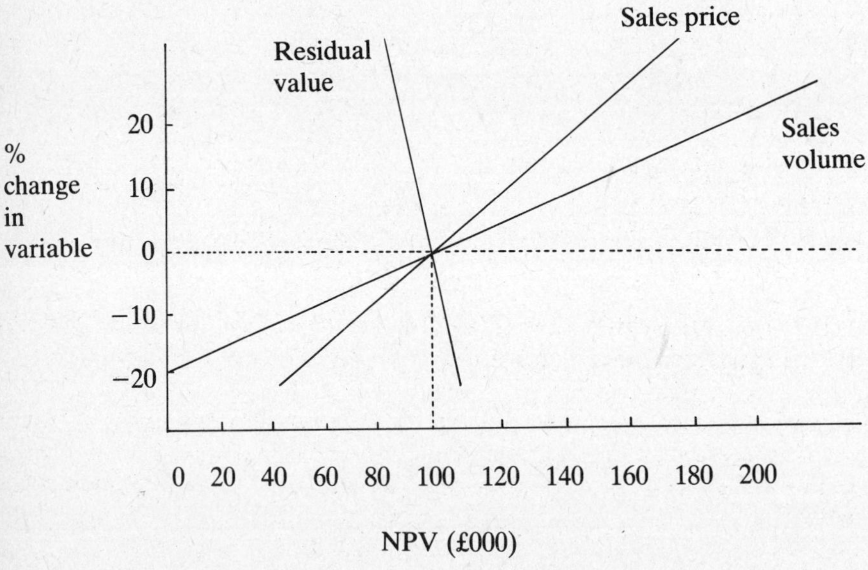

Figure 2   Graphic presentation of sensitivity analysis

From the table and graph it can be seen that sales volume is the most sensitive variable and the residual value the least. It does not matter, therefore, if the forecast future residual value has a high degree of error since the effect on the decision criterion is comparatively very small. The forecasters can thus concentrate their efforts into providing estimates which are as accurate as possible for the remaining two variables where a small degree of variation produces a significant effect on the resultant NPV.

Break-even analysis Another technique for determining the critical variables that are involved in a project has been put forward by B. Prodham 'Sensitivity analysis to identify key factors in capital budgeting', *Management Accounting*, November 1974. He suggests that by giving each variable in turn the value necessary for the project to break even, a margin of safety can be assigned to it, and thus a sensitivity ranking.

Example 3   Determining the critical variables using break-even analysis

Variables	Value given (A)	Value to break even (B)	Margin of safety (%) $\dfrac{A-B}{A} \times 100$	Sensitivity ranking
1 Sales volume (tons)	20,000	11,595	42	3
2 Selling price (£/ton)	5	4.52	9.6	1
3 Variable cost (£/ton)	3	3.48	16	2
4 Fixed costs (£ p.a.)	10,000	26,810	168	6
5 Project life (years)	5	2	60	4
6 Cost of capital (%)	10	54	440	7
7 Initial investment (£)	50,000	114,366	129	5
NPV (using firm's cost of capital) (£)	64,366			

If the firm therefore wished to concentrate on the three most sensitive factors so that variances could be minimised, variables 1, 2 and 3 would be chosen.

Disadvantages of simulation techniques Both of these methods, although recognising that estimates are unlikely to be exactly met, have a number of disadvantages relating to the ability of the manager to build an appropriate model:

(a) Whilst sensitivity analysis shows the effect of changes in the variables, the likelihood of each containing an estimation error is not normally explicitly considered. For instance, is the probability of a 20% error in estimating sales volume equal to the probability of a 20% error in estimating the residual value?

(b) The variables may not be independent of each other. If the selling price goes down, sales volume may go up. These techniques may not allow for this, if the model does not explicitly deal with these relationships.

(c) The value of a parameter one year may depend on the value of the same parameter in previous years. Sensitivity analysis, however, completely ignores autocorrelation.

(d) Only a small number of changes can be dealt with manually. If a more realistic comparison to the real world is to be achieved, much more complex calculations are necessary to incorporate (a), (b) and (c). This requires computer simulation.

Treatment of uncertainty by probabilistic analysis

What follows is a detailed treatment of uncertainty. The non-mathematical student can turn to the paragraph on 'Ultimate Decision' (below).

To reiterate, in the real world any investment decisions that are based on a single net present value or internal rate of return are unsatisfactory, because there will almost certainly be factors occurring beyond the company's control which will effect the forecast variables that were used to calculate the decision criteria. The aim of probabilistic analysis is to provide some assessment of the range of possible outcomes which may occur as the result of this, and thus provide additional information for the ultimate decision-maker.

Mean and standard deviation estimates — the use of confidence intervals
This statistical technique offers one approach to probabilistic analysis.

If the mean and the standard deviation of the distribution of all the possible residual net cash flows of a project due to uncertainty can be established, it is possible not only to calculate the probabilities of various results being achieved, but also to estimate an interval, or range, showing the degree of confidence one has in such a calculation. To enable such calculations to be made, however, an assumption regarding the probability distribution of the cash flows must first be introduced. In the following text a normal distribution has been applied to all computations, though in practice the choice lies solely with the decision-maker.

In procedures that do not attempt to quantify the uncertainty associated with a project, a single forecast of the residual net cash flow only is put forward. This estimate is still required for this technique and is adopted as the mean value.

Once the value of the mean has been determined the next requirement is to obtain some measure of the expected variability of the distribution around it; that is, calculate the standard deviation. As a rule, the larger the standard deviation value, the greater the variation and hence the uncertainty involved in a project (see Figure 3).

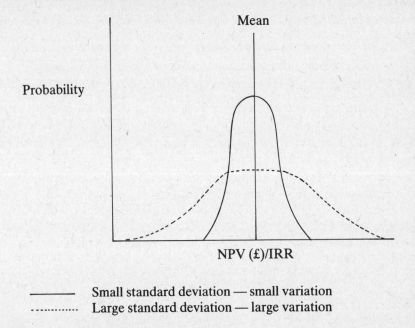

─────── Small standard deviation — small variation
············· Large standard deviation — large variation

Figure 3   Effect of standard deviation

How can the standard deviation of all the possible residual net cash flows which may occur from an investment be calculated? One method would be to ask the question: 'What is the range on either side of the mean value that there is an even chance that the actual result will lie within?' If the reply, for example, was £9,000-£11,000, (the mean being equal to £10,000 because we are assuming a normal distribution), then from normal area tables where it is known that 68% of the probability distribution will lie within the mean ±1 standard deviation:

$$11,000 - 10,000 = \sigma$$
$$\sigma = £1,000$$

where σ = standard deviation.

Once the mean and standard deviation are known it is possible to obtain a probability distribution of the decision criteria in the following way:

$$\text{NPV} = \sum_{t=0}^{t=n} \frac{C_t}{(1+r)^t}$$

where C_t = most likely cash flow through time
          r = cost of capital

This gives the expected value of NPV since the most likely values of the tth cash flows have been used.

However, by restating this to take into consideration that the cash flows are random variables with a known mean, μ_t, and known standard deviation, σ_t, the formula becomes:

$$\text{NPV} = \sum_{t=0}^{t=n} \frac{X_t}{(1+r)^t}$$

where X_t is a random variable with a normal distribution and hence NPV is a derived random variable with a statistical distribution; the central limit theorem tells us that this is a normal distribution whose mean is the sum of means and whose variance is the sum of variances.

If $X_0, X_1, X_2, \ldots, X_n$ are assumed to be mutually independent*, then:

$$\text{NPV} = \sum_{t=0}^{t=n} \frac{\mu_t}{(1+r)^t}$$

and by taking the statistical sum of $\sigma_0, \sigma_1, \sigma_2, \ldots, \sigma_n$:

$$\sigma^2\text{NPV} = \sum_{t=0}^{t=n} \left[\frac{\sigma_t}{(1+r)^t} \right]^2$$

$$\sigma^2\text{NPV} = \sum_{t=0}^{t=n} \frac{\sigma_t^2}{(1+r)^{2t}}$$

*It is possible to incorporate into the analysis the assumption that the cash flows are perfectly correlated (i.e., errors in one direction in any year give errors in the same direction in the following years) or a combination of both (partial dependence), but this has the effect of making the method and calculations more complex and for simplicity only mutual independence has been assumed.

Having thus defined the probability distribution of the NPV in terms of μNPV and σNPV it is possible by applying the normal distribution tables to arrive at the probabilities of achieving various results.

Example 4 Consider the following:

Forecast data for an investment project using a 10% discount rate

Year	0	1	2	3	4
μ_t (£)	−100,000	40,000	35,000	25,000	25,000
σ_t (£)	—	3,000	4,000	5,000	6,500
10% discount factor for μ_t	1	0.909	0.826	0.751	0.683
10% discount factor squared for σ_t	1	0.826	0.683	0.564	0.466

$$\mu\text{NPV} = \sum_{t=0}^{t=4} \frac{\mu_t}{(1+0.1)^t}$$

$$= -100,000 + 36,360 + 28,910 + 18,775 + 17,075$$
$$= £1,120$$

$$\sigma^2\text{NPV} = \sum_{t=0}^{t=4} \frac{\sigma_t^2}{(1+0.1)^{2t}}$$

$$\sigma\text{NPV} = \sqrt{(7,434,000 + 10,928,000 + 14,100,000 + 19,688,500)}$$
$$= £7,222$$

From this additional information it is now possible to calculate the specific probability of an outcome occurring. For example, the probability of the NPV being greater than zero can be determined thus:

$$Z = \frac{x - \mu}{\sigma}$$

$$= \frac{0 - 1,120}{7,222}$$

$$= -0.155$$

$$P(\text{NPV} > 0) = \Phi(Z)$$

$$= \Phi(-0.155)$$

$$= 1 - \Phi(0.155) \qquad (\text{since } \Phi(-Z) = 1 - \Phi(Z))$$

$$= 1 - 0.4384$$

$$= 0.5616$$

By using the normal distribution tables, therefore, it is found that this investment project has a probability of 0.5616 of yielding a NPV greater than zero. It can be seen then, that by applying this technique, the ultimate decision-maker can be provided with a quantitative summary of the forecaster's assessment of the project's uncertainty.

From the normal distribution where $Z = (x - \mu)/\sigma$ it can be seen that approximately 68% of sample observations will lie between $-1 \leqslant Z \leqslant 1$ and that approximately 95% of observations will lie between $-2 \leqslant Z \leqslant 2$ and so on. This can be applied to the decision criteria to estimate a range of values, for which a certain degree of confidence in the range can be assumed.

For instance, at the 99% level of confidence the range of NPVs for the investment project in example 4 would be:

sample mean $\pm$ (sample standard deviation $\times$ 2.575)
$= 1,120 \pm (7,222 \times 2.575)$
$= -$ £17,477 to £19,717

This means that the NPV for the project would be between $-$£17,477 and £19,717, and that this estimation should be true 99 times out of 100.

Again then, by determining the mean and standard deviation values and applying the normal distribution tables, more relevant information has been given to the decision-maker, thus helping to provide a more rational basis on which to make a decision.

It should be remembered, however, that although probabilistic analysis is a very useful appraisal tool, the probabilities from which the mean and standard deviations are determined are subjective assessments based on the information that is available, and may therefore not necessarily be correct. It is this stumbling block of having to provide sufficiently accurate forecast data (the responsibility of management) so as to eliminate unnecessary errors, that prevents the wider-scale acceptance and use of this technique in practice.

THE ULTIMATE DECISION

All the methods of incorporating the effects of uncertainty into the appraisal process that have so far been discussed, are essentially means of providing the decision-maker with more information. They do not assist in the actual decision-taking nor do they ensure that rational, consistent decisions are made. The following sections contain a number of techniques that have been developed and which will, if applied correctly, give such decisions, providing some prior preferences reflecting the decision-maker's attitude towards risk are established.

Expected monetary value

The result of the probabilistic analysis discussed in the previous section would be a statement of the possible outcomes of all the proposed projects together with their associated probabilities. Using this information a relatively simple decision rule would be to accept the investment with the highest expected return.

Example 5   Consider the following two projects:

Expected value comparison of two projects

Project A:

NPV (£)	Probability	Expected NPV (£)
5,000	0.1	500
15,000	0.2	3,000
20,000	0.4	8,000
30,000	0.2	6,000
35,000	0.1	3,500
Total expected net present value		21,000
Standard deviation		8,306

Project B:

NPV (£)	Probability	Expected NPV (£)
−100,000	0.1	−10,000
26,250	0.8	21,000
100,000	0.1	10,000
Total expected net present value		21,000
Standard deviation		45,937

In this example an investor who is indifferent towards risk will regard both projects as equally acceptable. However, project B has a greater variability of return and in addition the possibility of a substantial loss. How a firm would react to such information would be dependent on its attitude towards risk (i.e., its risk preference). A risk-averter would normally choose project A. A risk-taker would normally choose project B. It is for this reason that the individual firm's risk preference should be made as explicit as possible in the decision making process.

Decision tree analysis

This type of analysis can be used when management believes that there will be several decision points or alternative chance events occurring in the development and/or implementation of a project. It is particularly useful when the decision-maker is faced with the problem of whether or not to purchase more information about the likely outcome of an investment, so as to reduce the degree of risk attached to that decision. Obviously this information is not obtained for free — in fact it may be very costly. However, without this information a wrong decision, which subsequently turns out to be far more expensive, may be made.

A decision tree is a formal representation of this, and any other alternatives that may occur during the project's life. At each point different paths can be chosen, and, since a probability of success is assigned to each, by multiplying all the probabilities along any route from origin to completion, the expected return of each alternative can be determined. A ranking of the available decision alternatives can then be achieved in terms of expected monetary pay-off.

Example 6   A firm in the music business is deciding whether before it markets a new record some preliminary market research should be undertaken. The management feel that sufficient market research will cost £1,000,000 and the chances of it giving either a favourable or unfavourable result are 4/5 and 1/5 respectively. Table 2 shows how the profit that the new record will earn is dependent on its position in the total market records 'best sellers' list, and also the probability that it will achieve that position.

Table 2   Profit depending on 'best seller' list placing and its related probability

Record placing	Profit (£ million)	Probability (no market research)	Probability (market research gives a favourable result)
Top 10	5	1/20	2/20
Top 20 but not in Top 10	3	2/20	6/20
Top 50 but not in Top 20	1	4/20	6/20
Top 100 but not in Top 50	0	5/20	4/20
Not in top 100	−2	8/20	2/20

The decision tree facing this firm can be represented as shown in Figure 4.

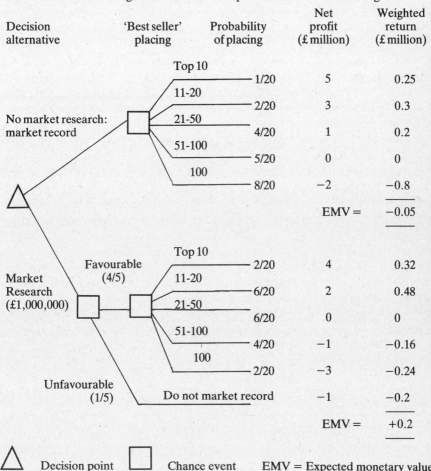

Decision alternative	'Best seller' placing	Probability of placing	Net profit (£ million)	Weighted return (£ million)

No market research: market record

Top 10	1/20	5	0.25
11-20	2/20	3	0.3
21-50	4/20	1	0.2
51-100	5/20	0	0
100	8/20	−2	−0.8

EMV = −0.05

Market Research (£1,000,000)

Favourable (4/5)

Top 10	2/20	4	0.32
11-20	6/20	2	0.48
21-50	6/20	0	0
51-100	4/20	−1	−0.16
100	2/20	−3	−0.24

Unfavourable (1/5)   Do not market record   −1   −0.2

EMV = +0.2

△ Decision point   ☐ Chance event   EMV = Expected monetary value

Figure 4   Decision tree of record company

From these results it can be seen that on the basis of expected monetary values, the decision of whether or not to release the record on to the market would be delayed until some preliminary market research had been undertaken.

Obviously this is an oversimplified example. In the real world the decision tree facing a firm will be much more complex than this, probably containing several more decision points and chance events.

It is possible to modify the decision tree to give results in terms of present values. In the case of the record firm this was not necessary since the length of time between the implementation and completion of the project was not sufficiently great. However, if the project has a life of more than one year, management may feel it necessary to take into account the time value of money. This can be done in the following way.

Example 7 Assume Figure 5 represents one of the possible decision tree paths of a project under consideration.

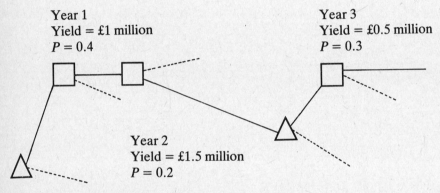

Figure 5 A single decision tree path

The weighted 'present value' return of this particular path can be determined by discounting each yield (i.e., the net cash flow) at the appropriate discount rate and then summing them all together, as in Table 3.

Table 3 Weighted 'present value' return of a single decision tree path

Year	Net cash flow (£ million)	Discount factor (10%)	Present value (£ million)	Probability	Weighted 'present value' return (£ million)
1	1	0.909	0.909	0.4	0.3636
2	1.5	0.826	1.239	0.2	0.2478
3	0.5	0.751	0.3755	0.3	0.11265
					0.72405

To find the weighted 'present value' return for the whole project (i.e., its expected monetary value in present value terms) each path would be calculated using the same procedure and the final result then computed as normal.

In the case of larger and more complex projects a further refinement to the decision tree approach — the inclusion of continuous probability distributions — may be worth considering. However, one of the problems faced in such a network diagram is that as the number of decision points and chance event points increases, the more difficult it becomes to interpret and calculate manually. It would, however, be dangerous to reduce the number of branches for the sake of simplicity and risk the removal of a realistic representation of the true complexity of the situation. It is here that the computer can become useful.

Figure 6 shows the replacement of the branches emanating from a chance event with a continuous probability distribution. This could be applied to the whole decision tree if required.

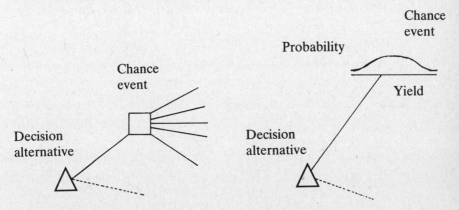

Figure 6   Probability of a chance event occurring as a continuous distribution

By using a computer simulation model, a random selection of results can be obtained. This will not only give an expected monetary value, but will also reflect the full range of possible results together with the probability of attaining more or less than such results, thus adding a greater 'feel' for the potential to be gained from a course of action and its attendant risk. Another useful factor obtainable from such a computer model is that it can facilitate the establishment of the key investment or cash flow figures by means of sensitivity analysis.

Decision tree analysis has one advantage over the expected monetary value technique, in that it takes into account the opportunity that, if one decision is taken, it can be modified later either to increase its profits or to reduce its losses. It is this implicit flexibility that has made Magee a strong advocate of decision tree analysis. He wrote:

The unique feature of the decision tree is that it allows management to combine analytical techniques such as discounted cash flow and present value methods with a clear portrayal of the impact of future decision alternatives and events. Using the decision tree, management can consider various courses of action with greater ease and clarity. The interactions between present decision alternatives, uncertain events, and future choices and their results then become more visible. [J. R. Magee 'Decision trees for decision models' *Harvard Business Review*, July-August 1964.]

However, because decision tree analysis is basically an extension of the expected monetary value technique it suffers from the same problem of not being directly able to incorporate individual risk preferences.

In conclusion, therefore, although its use as a visual aid for the explanation of a complex plan of action to management is justified, the above limitation, and also that of obtaining accurate representative probabilities, must be borne in mind.

INFLATION

Effect on the investment decision

Inflation may be defined as the rate of change of price increases. It is, however, important at the outset to make a distinction between general price inflation and relative price inflation, since each is dealt with differently in the capital budgeting decision.

General price inflation refers to an increase in the average price level of all the goods and services that are available, and has the effect of reducing the purchasing power of money. Relative price inflation occurs when the prices of specific goods and services which are of particular importance to the decision-maker (i.e., those that affect the firm) are increasing at a rate not equal to that of general price inflation.

Example 8   In order to show how the impact of both types of inflation can be taken into account, consider the project shown in Table 4 which is under review by ZZZ Ltd, a firm with a 10% cost of capital.

Table 4   Present value of a project having a four-year life and initial outlay of £50,000

Year	Revenue (£)	Cost (£)	Profit (£)	Discount factor (10%)	Present value (£)
0	—	50,000	(50,000)	1	(50,000)
1	50,000	25,000	25,000	0.909	22,725
2	50,000	25,000	25,000	0.826	20,650
3	50,000	25,000	25,000	0.751	18,775
4	50,000	25,000	25,000	0.683	17,075
					29,225

ZZZ Ltd believes that its revenue will rise by 8% annually in keeping with the level of general price inflation, but is not sure whether its costs will increase by 8% or 12% and therefore wishes to determine what effect both of these outcomes will have on the present value of the project.

(a) General price inflation, i.e., revenues and costs increase by 8% annually. The effects of this are shown in Table 5. As can be seen, in periods of general price inflation whether its effects on revenues and costs are incorporated into the analysis or not, no difference is made to the resultant present value. This alternative can therefore be ignored.

(b) Relative price inflation, i.e., revenue increases by 8% annually and costs by 12%. The effects of this are shown in Table 6. Providing then that the inflation adjusted profit is deflated into current money terms, relative price inflation is quite easy to deal with. Here, as expected, since costs have risen by a rate greater than that of revenue the present value of the project is reduced.

From a technical point of view, therefore, inflation does not seem to present a problem. However, it should be remembered that predicting the actual levels of inflation does. All forecasts, no matter how complex their compilation, are subject to error and this is certainly no exception.

Table 5   Present value of project in period of 8% general price inflation

Year	Revenue (8% inflation adjusted) (£)	Costs (8% inflation adjusted) (£)	Inflation adjusted profit (£)	Deflator 8%	Profit in current money terms (£)	Discount factor (10%)	Present value (£)
0	—	50,000	(50,000)	1	(50,000)	1	(50,000)
1	54,000	27,000	27,000	0.926	25,000	0.909	22,725
2	58,320	29,160	29,160	0.857	25,000	0.826	20,650
3	62,986	31,493	31,493	0.794	25,000	0.751	18,775
4	68,024	34,012	34,012	0.735	25,000	0.683	17,075
							————
							29,225

Table 6   Present value of project in period of relative price inflation

Year	Revenue (8% inflation adjusted) (£)	Costs (12% inflation adjusted) (£)	Inflation adjusted profit (£)	Deflator 8%	Profit in current money terms (£)	Discount factor (10%)	Present value (£)
0	—	50,000	(50,000)	1	(50,000)	1	(50,000)
1	54,000	28,000	26,000	0.926	24,076	0.909	21,885
2	58,320	31,360	26,960	0.857	23,105	0.826	19,085
3	62,986	35,123	27,863	0.794	22,123	0.751	16,614
4	68,024	39,338	28,686	0.735	21,084	0.683	14,400
							————
							21,984

Effect on the cost of borrowing

One 'side effect' of inflation is that it reduces the real cost of borrowing. Since many firms will take out loans to finance their investment projects it may be useful to explain briefly how this can occur.

Example 9   Assume a firm borrows £10,000 over one year at an interest rate of 10% per annum. If in this one year period there is no inflation then the amount paid back is:

10,000   + 1,000   = £11,000
(initial loan)   (interest)

If, however, the level of inflation is 8% then the amount paid back in real money terms is:

$$11,000 \times \frac{1}{1.08} = £10,185$$

which is £815 less.

If for some reason the inflation rate had been greater than the interest rate then the real cost of borrowing would in fact be negative.

ASSET REPLACEMENT DECISIONS

A company may buy a new fixed asset either to replace an existing, ageing asset, or else to expand its business. Some replacement assets might have a greater production/operating capacity than their existing equivalent, so that both expansion and replacement occurs with the same purchase.

The major problem with replacement is not so much 'should the asset be replaced?', but rather 'when?' or 'how frequently?' To evaluate a replacement decision DCF techniques should be used because the element of time is involved and therefore the time value of money cannot be ignored.

The factors involved in replacement decisions are:

(a)   operating and maintenance costs;
(b)   capital costs;
(c)   realisable values;
(d)   taxation and investment incentives;
(e)   opportunity costs;
(f)   inflation.

Optimal life analysis

Optimal life analysis is a special case of mutually exclusive projects involving the evaluation of 'when' an asset should be replaced. For example, what is the optimal life of an aeroplane or a road vehicle? Here the projects may have a virtually unlimited life if all their various components are replaced when they wear out, but there must be a point in time when it is more economical simply to purchase a whole new asset than continually to replace parts of the existing one.

There are two ways of treating this situation which ensure that like is compared with like:

(a) Take the least common multiple of the possible lives (e.g. six years if lives of two and three years are to be compared) and accept the life which gives the lowest net present value of costs over this period.

(b) Convert the net present value of the costs for each possible life into an annuity, then simply compare the annuities.

Replacement analysis

DCF techniques can be used in the replacement decision, enabling a company to plan ahead for a replacement cycle that minimises the operating costs of a particular asset.

We can use the theoretical model of A. J. Merrett and A. Sykes *The Finance and Analysis of Capital Projects* 2nd ed, 1973 to determine the minimum-cost operating cycles; the formula for which is:

$$V_n = \frac{C - R_n - S_n}{1 - (1 - r)^{-n}}$$

where V = cost of cycle
  n = number of years
  C = capital cost
  R = annual operating cost
  S = residual value
  r = discount rate

The objective is to calculate the operating cycle which minimises these costs. However, in comparing different operating cycles we cannot use total cost, which obviously increases with the length of the cycle. The desired replacement cycle is the one with the minimum 'annual cost'.

The relationship between the total cost of an operating cycle (V_n) and its resulting annual cost (AC) is given as:

$$AC = V_n \times CRF_{rn}$$

where CRF_{rn} is the capital recovery factor for a discount rate of r over an operating cycle of n years. This factor can be obtained from most sets of financial tables and is the reciprocal of the sum of the discount factors.

The optimal replacement cycle is that cycle with minimum total annual cost. Total annual cost comprises maintenance costs and capital cost and, as already mentioned, as the replacement cycle lengthens, maintenance costs increase whilst capital costs decline. The interaction of these two cost profiles determines the minimum-cost replacement cycle.

Advantages of a planned replacement cycle

A rational replacement policy has a number of advantages:

    (a) Total operating costs can be minimised.

    (b) The company has time to negotiate the best terms and best acquisition method for the replacement.

    (c) Repair costs can be cut back to essential items only as an asset nears replacement, thus saving more money.

    (d) Cash flows can be planned.

    (e) There is time to study alternative assets to replace those presently in use and decide on a replacement best suited to the company's needs.

    (f) There is time to plan the replacement to cause minimum disruption.

Clearly the advantages of a planned policy of asset replacement are substantial.

Technological change and inflation affect replacement cycles, such that the planned minimum annual cost replacement cycle may no longer be the optimum point at which to replace the asset. Generally, technological change implies that assets should be replaced earlier than the minimum annual cost point, whereas inflation implies that assets should be replaced later than that point.

Example 10 Little and Co are engaged in the manufacture of plumbing components, one of which, the Bend, requires the use of a special machine. Details of the Bend are as follows:

Selling price per unit	20p
Variable costs per unit	12p
Allocated fixed overheads per unit	4p

The above costings do not include running costs or depreciation of the machine. Running costs are detailed below, and depreciation is charged on a straight-line basis — details of cost and scrap values are given below.

Little and Co are considering how often to replace the special machine in view of the fact that it has a limited life, and its productive capacity declines as it gets older.

Details of productive capacities and running costs for successive years of the machine's life are as follows:

Year	Productive capacity (No. of Bends)	Running costs (at current prices) (£)
1	750,000	8,000
2	750,000	8,500
3	600,000	10,000
4	500,000	12,000

New machines cost £75,000 currently, and their resale values are:

Age (years)	Resale value (at current price) (£)
1	50,000
2	30,000
3	20,000
4	15,000

Running costs are independent of the number of Bends manufactured.

Assume all costs and revenues are paid or received in cash at the end of the year to which they relate, with the exception of the initial machine cost which is paid immediately on purchase. All costs and revenues are expressed in current prices. Inflation is expected to be at an annual uniform rate of 5%. Little and Co have an annual cost of capital of 15.5%.

Whether or not Little and Co should replace the machine every one, two, three or four years is calculated in the following way.

On the basis that fixed overheads are fixed in total, calculations have been done on the basis of a contribution per unit of 8p. Since all flows are at current prices and inflate at 5% p.a. with the cost of capital 15.5% p.a., all calculations have been performed using the effective rate of 10%, since $r = (1.15/1.05) - 1 = 0.10$ (to 2 decimal places).

1-year replacement cycle:

Year			10%	PV £
0	Cost	(75,000)	1	(75,000)
1	Sales	60,000		
1	Running costs	(8,000)	0.90909	47,273
1	Scrap	50,000	0.90909	45,455
				17,728

Therefore equivalent annual receipt is:

$$\frac{17,728}{\text{1-year ADF @ 10\%}} = \frac{17,728}{0.90909} = £19,501 \text{ p.a.}$$

2-year replacement cycle:

Year			10%	PV £
0	Cost	(75,000)	1	(75,000)
1	Net inflow	52,000	$1/1.1$	47,273
2	Net inflow	51,500	$1/1.1^2$	42,562
2	Scrap	30,000	$1/1.1^2$	24,793
				39,628

Therefore equivalent annual receipt is:

$$\frac{39,628}{\text{2-year ADF @ 10\%}} = \frac{39,628}{1.735537} = £22,833 \text{ p.a.}$$

3-year replacement cycle:

Year			10%	PV £
0	Cost	(75,000)		(75,000)
1	Net inflow	52,000		47,273
2	Net inflow	51,000		42,562
3	Net inflow	38,000	$1/1.1^3$	28,550
3	Scrap	20,000	$1/1.1^3$	15,026
				58,411

Therefore equivalent annual receipt is:

$$\frac{58,411}{\text{3-year ADF} @ 10\%} = \frac{58,411}{2.48685} = £23,488 \text{ p.a.}$$

4-year replacement cycle:

Year			10%	PV £
0	Cost	(75,000)		(75,000)
1	Net inflow	52,000		47,273
2	Net inflow	51,000		42,562
3	Net inflow	38,000		28,550
4	Net inflow	28,000	$1/1.1^4$	19,124
4	Scrap	15,000	$1/1.1^4$	10,245
				72,754

Therefore equivalent annual receipt is:

$$\frac{72,754}{\text{4-year ADF} @ 10\%} = \frac{72,754}{3.16986} = £22,952 \text{ p.a.}$$

On the basis of the above calculations, it is apparent that the machine should be replaced every three years.

LEASE OR BUY DECISIONS

In decisions of this nature, we are reviewing different time patterns of expenditure to discover which is the least expensive.

Example ABC Limited has decided to install a new milling machine. The machine costs £20,000 and would last five years with a trade-in value of £4,000 at the end of the fifth year. The company's cost of capital is 12%.

As alternatives to outright purchase the company could buy the machine on hire purchase, paying an initial deposit of £6,000, and instalments of £4,000 per annum at the end of the next five years; or it could lease the machine at a cost of £4,800 per annum for five years payable at the beginning of each year. Under this alternative there would be savings in insurance and servicing of £500 per annum. What is the better alternative?

On the facts given, the annual cash flows and their present values at 12% would be as follows:

Year	Discount factor	Outright purchase Cash flows	Outright purchase Present vlaue	Hire purchase Cash flows	Hire purchase Present value	Leasing Cash flows	Leasing Present value
0	1.00	(20,000)	(20,000)	(6,000)	(6,000)	(4,800)	(4,800)
1	.89			(4,000)		(4,300)*	
2	.80			(4,000)		(4,300)	
3	.71			(4,000)	(12,160)	(4,300)	(13,072)
4	.64			(4,000)		(4,300)	
5	.57	4,000	2,280	0**		500	285
Net present value			(17,720)		(18,160)		(17,587)

Notes: * £4,800 less savings £500.
            **£4,000 less residual value £4,000.
            Leasing has the lowest cost, and is the preferred alternative.

Where only two alternative methods of financing the acquisition were under consideration it would be possible of course to calculate the incremental cash flows and just discount those.

One of the main features of these decisions, the amount and timing of tax relief, has been omitted from the above simple example. In practice this would always be taken into account.

It is assumed that the leasing of this machine is the most profitable way of using the £20,000 outlay, this may not be the case, and one ought to look at the alternative uses of the money before taking a final decision. It is also important to remember other issues such as the liquidity of the company, any maintenance element in the leasing agreement and technical obsolescence.

Present value of 1
at compound interest $(1+r)^{-n}$

Years (n)	Interest rates (r)									
	1	2	3	4	5	6	7	8	9	10
1	0.9901	0.9804	0.9709	0.9615	0.9524	0.9434	0.9346	0.9259	0.9174	0.9091
2	0.9803	0.9612	0.9426	0.9246	0.9070	0.8900	0.8734	0.8573	0.8417	0.8264
3	0.9706	0.9423	0.9151	0.8890	0.8638	0.8396	0.8163	0.7938	0.7722	0.7513
4	0.9610	0.9238	0.8885	0.8548	0.8227	0.7921	0.7629	0.7350	0.7084	0.6830
5	0.9515	0.9057	0.8626	0.8219	0.7835	0.7473	0.7139	0.6806	0.6499	0.6209
6	0.9420	0.8880	0.8375	0.7903	0.7462	0.7050	0.6663	0.6302	0.5963	0.5645
7	0.9327	0.8706	0.8131	0.7599	0.7107	0.6651	0.6227	0.5835	0.5470	0.5132
8	0.9235	0.8535	0.7894	0.7307	0.6768	0.6274	0.5820	0.5403	0.5019	0.4665
9	0.9143	0.8368	0.7664	0.7026	0.6446	0.5919	0.5439	0.5002	0.4604	0.4241
10	0.9053	0.8203	0.7441	0.6756	0.6139	0.5584	0.5083	0.4632	0.4224	0.3855
11	0.8963	0.8043	0.7224	0.6496	0.5847	0.5268	0.4751	0.4289	0.3875	0.3505
12	0.8874	0.7885	0.7014	0.6246	0.5568	0.4970	0.4440	0.3971	0.3555	0.3186
13	0.8787	0.7730	0.6810	0.6006	0.5303	0.4688	0.4150	0.3677	0.3262	0.2897
14	0.8700	0.7579	0.6611	0.5775	0.5051	0.4423	0.3878	0.3405	0.2992	0.2633
15	0.8613	0.7430	0.6419	0.5553	0.4810	0.4173	0.3624	0.3152	0.2745	0.2394
16	0.8528	0.7284	0.6232	0.5339	0.4581	0.3936	0.3387	0.2919	0.2519	0.2176
17	0.8444	0.7142	0.6050	0.5134	0.4363	0.3714	0.3166	0.2703	0.2311	0.1978
18	0.8360	0.7002	0.5874	0.4936	0.4155	0.3503	0.2959	0.2502	0.2120	0.1799
19	0.8277	0.6864	0.5703	0.4746	0.3957	0.3305	0.2765	0.2317	0.1945	0.1635
20	0.8195	0.6730	0.5537	0.4564	0.3769	0.3118	0.2584	0.2145	0.1784	0.1486
25	0.7795	0.6095	0.4776	0.3751	0.2953	0.2330	0.1842	0.1460	0.1160	0.0923
30	0.7419	0.5521	0.4120	0.3083	0.2314	0.1741	0.1314	0.0994	0.0754	0.0573
35	0.7059	0.5000	0.3554	0.2534	0.1813	0.1301	0.0937	0.0676	0.0490	0.0356
40	0.6717	0.4529	0.3066	0.2083	0.1420	0.0872	0.0668	0.0450	0.0318	0.0221
45	0.6391	0.4102	0.2644	0.1712	0.1113	0.0727	0.0476	0.0313	0.0207	0.0137
50	0.6080	0.3715	0.2251	0.1407	0.0872	0.0543	0.0339	0.0213	0.0134	0.0085

Years (n) Interest rates (r)

Years (n)	11	12	13	14	15	16	17	18	19	20
1	0.9009	0.8929	0.8850	0.8772	0.8696	0.8621	0.8547	0.8475	0.8403	0.8333
2	0.8116	0.7972	0.7831	0.7695	0.7561	0.7432	0.7305	0.7182	0.7062	0.6944
3	0.7312	0.7118	0.6931	0.6750	0.6575	0.6407	0.6244	0.6086	0.5934	0.5787
4	0.6587	0.6355	0.6133	0.5921	0.5718	0.5523	0.5337	0.5158	0.4987	0.4823
5	0.5935	0.5674	0.5428	0.5194	0.4972	0.4761	0.4561	0.4371	0.4190	0.4019
6	0.5346	0.5066	0.4803	0.4556	0.4323	0.4104	0.3898	0.3704	0.3521	0.3349
7	0.4817	0.4523	0.4251	0.3996	0.3759	0.3538	0.3332	0.3139	0.2959	0.2791
8	0.4339	0.4039	0.3762	0.3506	0.3269	0.3050	0.2848	0.2660	0.2487	0.2326
9	0.3909	0.3606	0.3329	0.3075	0.2843	0.2630	0.2434	0.2255	0.2090	0.1938
10	0.3522	0.3220	0.2946	0.2697	0.2472	0.2267	0.2080	0.1911	0.1756	0.1615
11	0.3173	0.2875	0.2607	0.2366	0.2149	0.1954	0.1778	0.1619	0.1476	0.1346
12	0.2858	0.2567	0.2307	0.2076	0.1869	0.1685	0.1520	0.1372	0.1240	0.1122
13	0.2575	0.2292	0.2042	0.1821	0.1625	0.1452	0.1299	0.1163	0.1042	0.0935
14	0.2320	0.2046	0.1807	0.1597	0.1413	0.1252	0.1110	0.0985	0.0876	0.0779
15	0.2090	0.1827	0.1599	0.1401	0.1229	0.1079	0.0949	0.0835	0.0736	0.0649
16	0.1883	0.1631	0.1415	0.1229	0.1069	0.0930	0.0811	0.0708	0.0618	0.0541
17	0.1696	0.1456	0.1252	0.1078	0.0929	0.0802	0.0693	0.0600	0.0520	0.0451
18	0.1528	0.1300	0.1108	0.0946	0.0808	0.0691	0.0592	0.0508	0.0437	0.0376
19	0.1377	0.1161	0.0981	0.0829	0.0703	0.0596	0.0506	0.0431	0.0367	0.0313
20	0.1240	0.1037	0.0868	0.0728	0.0611	0.0514	0.0433	0.0365	0.0308	0.0261
25	0.0736	0.0588	0.0471	0.0378	0.0304	0.0245	0.0197	0.0160	0.0129	0.0105
30	0.0437	0.0334	0.0256	0.0196	0.0151	0.0116	0.0090	0.0070	0.0054	0.0042
35	0.0259	0.0189	0.0139	0.0102	0.0075	0.0055	0.0041	0.0030	0.0023	0.0017
40	0.0154	0.0107	0.0075	0.0053	0.0037	0.0026	0.0019	0.0013	0.0010	0.0007
45	0.0091	0.0061	0.0041	0.0027	0.0019	0.0013	0.0008	0.0006	0.0004	0.0003
50	0.0054	0.0035	0.0022	0.0014	0.0008	0.0006	0.0004	0.0003	0.0002	0.0001

Years (n) Interest rates (r)

Years (n)	21	22	23	24	25	26	27	28	29	30
1	0.8264	0.8197	0.8130	0.8065	0.8000	0.7937	0.7874	0.7812	0.7752	0.7692
2	0.6830	0.6719	0.6610	0.6504	0.6400	0.6299	0.6200	0.6104	0.6009	0.5917
3	0.5645	0.5507	0.5374	0.5245	0.5120	0.4999	0.4882	0.4768	0.4659	0.4552
4	0.4665	0.4514	0.4369	0.4230	0.4096	0.3968	0.3844	0.3725	0.3611	0.3501
5	0.3855	0.3700	0.3552	0.3411	0.3277	0.3149	0.3027	0.2910	0.2799	0.2693
6	0.3186	0.3033	0.2888	0.2751	0.2621	0.2499	0.2383	0.2274	0.2170	0.2072
7	0.2633	0.2486	0.2348	0.2218	0.2097	0.1983	0.1877	0.1776	0.1682	0.1594
8	0.2176	0.2038	0.1909	0.1789	0.1678	0.1574	0.1478	0.1388	0.1304	0.1226
9	0.1799	0.1670	0.1552	0.1443	0.1342	0.1249	0.1164	0.1084	0.1011	0.0943
10	0.1486	0.1369	0.1262	0.1164	0.1074	0.0992	0.0916	0.0847	0.0784	0.0725
11	0.1228	0.1122	0.1026	0.0938	0.0859	0.0787	0.0721	0.0662	0.0607	0.0558
12	0.1015	0.0920	0.0834	0.0757	0.0687	0.0625	0.0568	0.0517	0.0471	0.0429
13	0.0839	0.0754	0.0678	0.0610	0.0550	0.0496	0.0447	0.0404	0.0365	0.0330
14	0.0693	0.0618	0.0551	0.0492	0.0440	0.0393	0.0352	0.0316	0.0283	0.0254
15	0.0573	0.0507	0.0448	0.0397	0.0352	0.0312	0.0277	0.0247	0.0219	0.0195
16	0.0474	0.0415	0.0364	0.0320	0.0281	0.0248	0.0218	0.0193	0.0170	0.0150
17	0.0391	0.0340	0.0296	0.0258	0.0225	0.0197	0.0172	0.0150	0.0132	0.0116
18	0.0323	0.0279	0.0241	0.0208	0.0180	0.0156	0.0135	0.0118	0.0102	0.0089
19	0.0267	0.0229	0.0196	0.0168	0.0144	0.0124	0.0107	0.0092	0.0079	0.0068
20	0.0221	0.0187	0.0159	0.0135	0.0115	0.0098	0.0084	0.0072	0.0061	0.0053
25	0.0085	0.0069	0.0057	0.0046	0.0038	0.0031	0.0025	0.0021	0.0017	0.0014
30	0.0033	0.0026	0.0020	0.0016	0.0012	0.0010	0.0009	0.0006	0.0005	0.0004
35	0.0013	0.0009	0.0007	0.0005	0.0004	0.0003	0.0002	0.0002	0.0001	0.0001
40	0.0005	0.0004	0.0002	0.0002	0.0001	0.0001	0.0001	0.0001	0.0000	0.0000
45	0.0002	0.0001	0.0001	0.0001	0.0000	0.0000	0.0000	0.0000	0.0000	0.0000
50	0.0001	0.0000	0.0000	0.0000	0.0000	0.0000	0.0000	0.0000	0.0000	0.0000

9 Dividend policy and share values

DIVIDENDS V RETAINED EARNINGS

Dividend policy determines the division of earnings between payments to shareholders and reinvestment in the firm. Retained earnings are one of the most significant sources of funds for financing corporate growth, but dividends constitute the cash flows that accrue to shareholders.

A number of considerations need to be made in deciding between dividends and retention:

(a) A company may only make a distribution out of profits available for this purpose (Companies Act 1985, s. 263(1)). These profits are defined as the sum of:

(i) Accumulated 'realised profits' not previously distributed or capitalised loss.

(ii) Accumulated 'realised losses' not previously written off in a reduction or reorganisation of capital.

The articles or memorandum of a company may be more restrictive in the definition of distributable profits.

There are certain legal restrictions on dividend payments which always apply.

(i) Dividends cannot be paid if this would result in a loss of solvency for the company.

(ii) A public company may make a distribution only if at the time the amount of its net assets is not less than the aggregate of its called-up share capital and undistributable reserves and then only if, and to the extent that, the distribution does not reduce the amount of the company's net assets to below that aggregate.

(iii) Losses of current assets in the current accounting period must be made good before a dividend can be paid.

(iv) Losses made in earlier accounting periods must be made good before a dividend can be paid.

(v) In the treatment of capital gains, a realised capital gain may be distributed, if the articles so permit, after a general bona fide appraisal of all assets.

(b) The *liquidity position* needs to be considered. Profits held as retained earnings are generally invested in assets required for the conduct of business. Retained earnings from preceding years are already invested in plant and equipment, stocks and other assets; they are not held as cash. Thus, although a firm has had a record of earnings, it may not be able to pay cash dividends because of its liquidity position. Indeed a growing firm, even a very profitable one, typically has a pressing need for funds. In such a situation the firm may elect not to pay cash dividends.

(c) The *rate of asset expansion* needs to be taken into account. The more rapid the rate at which the firm is growing, the greater will be its needs for financing asset expansion. The greater the future need for funds, the more likely the firm is to retain earnings rather than pay them out. If a firm seeks to raise funds externally, natural sources are the present shareholders who already know the company. Yet if earnings are paid out as dividends and are subjected to high personal income tax rates, only a portion of the earnings would be available for reinvestment.

(d) *Profit rate* also influences the dividend/retention policy. The rate of return on assets determines the relative attractiveness of paying out earnings in the form of dividends to shareholders who will use them elsewhere, compared with the productivity of their use in the present enterprise.

(e) The *stability of earnings* also affects the decision. If earnings are relatively stable, a firm is better able to predict what its future earnings will be. A stable firm is therefore more likely to pay out a higher percentage of its earnings than is a firm with fluctuating earnings. The unstable firm is not certain that in subsequent years the hoped-for earnings will be realised, so it is more likely to retain a high proportion of earnings.

(f) A final consideration is the *tax position of the shareholders*. The tax position of the owners of the company greatly influences the desire for dividends. For example, a company with a small number of shareholders in high tax brackets is likely to pay a relatively low dividend. The owners are interested in taking their income in the form of capital gains rather than as dividends, which are subject to higher personal income tax rates. The shareholders of a large company with many shareholders may, however, be interested in a high dividend pay-out. The subject of dividend policy and taxation will be considered more fully a little later.

INVESTMENT FINANCING

In a perfect capital market, retention financing and new equity financing are perfect substitutes, so that the choice between them does not affect the market value of the firm. The question of whether internal or external financing makes a difference in an imperfect market, therefore, depends, as a logical matter, on the market imperfections assumed to exist and on whether arrangements to overcome such imperfections can be found. Clearly, because retention financing has the feature of saving on underwriting costs, on these grounds considered by themselves the decision to finance internally should have a positive, although possibly small, effect on the firm's market value.

Another reason for favouring retention financing might be found in differing expectations regarding the company's earnings — prospective new investors might not be as optimistic as existing stockholders. For this reason a new issue might seem, at least in management's view, to have an excessively large implied capital cost. Even in the absence of differing expectations, the decision to sell new securities in imperfect markets can raise effective interest rates, at least for short periods of time. Accordingly, if this is a possibility, retention financing is likely to be cheaper than new issue financing for this reason also. Moreover, if at times financial market conditions are viewed as unfavourable by management, temporary use of retention financing might reduce finance costs by allowing the company to defer a new securities issue until such time as market conditions improve.

It must be noted that none of the foregoing arguments establishes that retention financing would have the net effect of increasing the firm's market value. Retention financing does reduce flotation costs but changes in dividend policies may have market value effects of their own when financial markets are imperfect.

INFLUENCES ON DIVIDEND POLICY

Dividend policy and external investment opportunities

It is arguable that if a shareholder in a company is aware of an opportunity for investing funds outside the company in order to gain a higher return than he receives from his present shares, then he will want a higher current dividend to provide him with the cash he needs to make the other investment. The argument is invalid, however, in that the shareholder can gain the necessary cash by selling his shares; or he can borrow using his shares as security. Also, if the company pays a higher current dividend, so that retained earnings are insufficient to finance all new projects which offer a positive NPV, it will need to raise or borrow new funds to make up the shortfall.

It can be argued that companies should ignore the external investment opportunities available to shareholders, and formulate a dividend policy which maximises the total wealth of the shares of the company itself. This will enable shareholders, by selling shares or by borrowing, to maximise their wealth from the combined investments both in the company and also outside it. It must be noted, however, that dividend policy cannot be ignored if shareholders are not able to sell shares easily or can only obtain a poor price for them. In such situations dividends are no longer merely one element of the shareholder's total wealth but become, perhaps, the shareholder's only source of funds. As a result, the existence of alternative opportunities outside the firm becomes important and must be taken directly into account by management.

Dividend policy and capital rationing

In a situation of capital rationing there are insufficient funds to undertake all the available, viable expenditure projects. In this situation the payment of a dividend, which reduces retained earnings, will only serve to exacerbate the shortage of funds. B. V. Carsberg in *Analysis for Investment Decisions* has argued that the logical optimum dividend policy is to pay no dividends at all but to reinvest all earnings because a company's value is only increased by undertaking projects with a positive net present value. In practice, however, the reduction of a dividend to zero is unusual because other policy considerations are thought to be of overriding importance for setting the level of dividend.

Dividend policy and personal taxation

As we noted earlier, there is at times a conflict of interest in large companies between shareholders in high income tax brackets. The former may prefer to see a low dividend pay-out and a high rate of earnings retention in the hope of an appreciation in the capital value of the company. The latter may prefer a relatively high dividend pay-out rate. The dividend policy of such a firm may be a compromise between a low and a high pay-out — an intermediate pay-out policy, those shareholders who seek income are likely to sell their shares over time and shift into higher yielding shares. Thus, at least to some extent, a firm's pay-out policy determines it shareholder types, as well as vice versa. This has been called the 'clientele influence' on dividend policy.

EFFECT OF DIVIDEND DECLARATIONS ON SHARE VALUES

A drop in the ex-dividend price of a share usually accompanies a dividend declaration. Dividend payments are financed out of earnings and therefore fewer funds will be available for reinvestment and consequently there will be a reduction in future earnings and dividends. The expected fall in the ex-dividend value of the shares should be equal to the amount of the current dividend if the following two conditions prevail:

(a) if the size of dividend does not affect the shareholder's view of risk; and
(b) if the company does not obtain new funds from other sources.

This can be explained by the fact that the future dividends which would have been earned by retaining the current dividend, when discounted at the shareholders' cost of capital to a present market value, would have the same value as the current dividend.

In practice, however, the fall in the exdividend value of a share is not equal to the amount of the current dividend, for two reasons:

(a) When a dividend is declared, the shareholders' view about the riskiness of the company might change, so that their cost of capital might rise or fall.

(b) The actual dividend declared may be different from the expected dividend, so that share prices would be boosted if actual dividends exceeded expectations, and conversely, if actual dividends fall short of expectations, the ex-dividend market value would fall by more than the size of the dividend.

J. T. S. Porterfield in 1965 in *Investment Decisions and Capital Costs* suggested that a dividend should be paid where the market value per share after the declaration of the dividend combined with the declared dividend is greater than or equal to the market value per share before declaration of dividend. This can be expressed as follows:

$V_1 + D_0 \geq V_0$
where V_0 = market value per share before declaration of the dividend
V_1 = market value per share after declaration of the dividend
D_0 = dividend per share declared

The Porterfield theory is illustrated more clearly in example 12.

Example 12   The shareholders of Wellington Rubber Co expect to earn a dividend of 25p per share each year into the foreseeable future. The current year's dividend is about to be declared.

The directors are considering making this year's dividend 35p but the consequent reduction in earnings would mean that in future years the dividend would only be 22p. The cost of capital of the shareholders is 15%. The question facing the directors, therefore, is whether the increase in current dividend is admissible.

The valuation of shares prior to dividend declaration is:

25p + 25p/0.15 = 191.6p

If a dividend of 35p is declared, and shareholders' expectations of future dividends fall to 22p, the value of shares cum dividend after the declaration should be:

35p + 22p/0.15 = 181.6p

Since the increase in dividend would reduce shareholder wealth by 10p the change in dividend policy is not admissible.

The Porterfield formula has its limitations; other factors affect the preference of shareholders for either current dividend or capital gain through retentions. These include investment opportunities outside the company, personal taxation of the shareholders, capital rationing, etc.

Finally, J. M. Samuels and F. M. Wilkes in *Management of Company Finance* put forward the suggestion that a changed dividend policy, i.e., the declaration of an actual dividend which is either higher or lower than the expected dividend, is desirable provided that:

$$V_1 + D_{0a} \geqslant V_0 + D_{0e}$$

$$\begin{aligned}
\text{where} \quad D_{0a} &= \text{actual dividend declared} \\
D_{0e} &= \text{expected dividend prior to the declaration} \\
V_0 &= \text{market price before declaration (ex dividend)} \\
V_1 &= \text{the market price after declaration (ex dividend)}
\end{aligned}$$

DIVIDEND POLICY AS A FINANCING DECISION

The dividend decision is actually a financing decision, since paying a dividend directly affects the firm's financing. We need to examine whether dividends can be an instrument for maximising shareholder wealth. We need to consider, therefore, whether dividends affect shareholder wealth or not, i.e., whether they are irrelevant or relevant.

Modigliani and Miller — the irrelevancy argument

M. H. Modigliani and F. Miller in 1961 in *Journal of Business* presented a cogent argument for the fact that the value of the firm is unaffected by dividend policy, i.e., dividends are irrelevant to shareholder wealth. They built their argument on a number of assumptions, the most critical of which were:

(a) no flotation or brokerage costs;
(b) no taxes;
(c) no uncertainty.

They also assumed for their argument the existence of two firms identical in every respect except for their dividend pay-out in the current time period. Their streams of future cash flows for operations are identical, their planned investment outlays are identical, and all future dividend payments from the second time period are also identical.

It was on the three key assumptions listed above that Modigliani and Miller argued that the value of the firm was not determined by the amount of dividends paid, but rather by the earning power of the projects in which the firm invested its money. They claimed that how the firm split its earnings between dividends and reinvestment had no direct effect on its value, since in a world without taxes there was no difference between dividends and capital gains. The argument used by Modigliani and Miller to support this key assumption is referred to as the 'clientele effect'. The clientele effect states that a firm will attract stockholders whose preferences with respect to the payment pattern and stability of dividends corresponds to the firm's payment pattern and stability of dividends. Since the shareholders, or the clientele, of the firm get what they expect, the value of the firm's stock is unaffected by changes in its dividend policy.

Modigliani and Miller's theory holds that the effect of dividends on share price is precisely offset by other forms of financing. The key to this is the belief that since the retention of earnings is a form of equity financing, the sale of common stock is an alternative source of equity financing. They argue that the negative effect of the dilution of earnings and ownership resulting from the sale of common stock on the stock's value is just offset by the positive effect of the dividends paid. Since they assume that there are no flotation or brokerage costs, the cost of raising common equity through the retention of earnings or the sale of new stock is in effect assumed to be the same. Their conclusion is that, given certain 'restrictive' assumptions, dividend policy is irrelevant since it has no effect on the market value of the firm.

In spite of the irrelevancy theory, Modigliani and Miller recognise that dividends do somehow affect stock prices; and therefore they suggest that the positive effects of dividend increases on stock prices are attributable not to the dividend itself, but rather to the informational content of dividends with respect to future earnings. The information provided by the dividends causes owners to bid up the price of the stock based on their expectations of future earnings. Modigliani and Miller's arguments lead one to believe that when acceptable investment opportunities are not available the firm should distribute the unneeded funds to the owners, who can invest the money in other firms having acceptable investment alternatives. This residual theory of dividends is consistent with Modigliani and Miller's dividend irrelevancy theory. It suggests that since, given certain assumptions, dividends are irrelevant to the firm's value, the firm does not need to have a 'dividend policy'.

The 'irrelevant dividend' argument can be expressed further by the following simple example.

Example 13 Workbooks plc, an all-equity company, pays a constant annual dividend of £2,000. The cost of capital is 10% and the company is about to declare its current dividend. The company is offered an investment which would cost £2,000 and earn £300 per annum in perpetuity. Since the project has a positive NPV of £1,000 when discounted at 10%, the company will wish to undertake it. Its options are:

(a) to withhold the current dividend, and finance the project from retained earnings of £2,000; or
(b) to pay the dividend, and obtain £2,000 from outside sources.

If the project is financed by retained earnings, the value of shares on the basis of expected future dividends will be:

$$2,000/0.1 + 300/0.1 = £23,000$$

If the project is financed by a new share issue, the value of the existing shares will be:

$$2,000 + (2,300 - D_n)/0.1$$

i.e., current dividend + future possible dividend $- D_n$, where D_n is the dividend paid in perpetuity on the new shares.

Since the cost of new equity will be 10%, the new shareholders should expect to receive exactly £200 per annum in perpetuity on their investment of £2,000 so that the value of the existing shares should be:

$$2,000 + \frac{(2,300 - 200)}{0.1} = 23,000$$

The relevance of dividends — the argument against Modigliani and Miller

Those who argue for the relevance of dividends suggest that without Modigliani and Miller's restrictive assumptions their argument collapses. They point to the fact that in reality the market is imperfect and investors in actuality do operate in a world of flotation costs, brokerage costs, taxes and uncertainty and it is therefore better to view the firm in the light of these factors.

If one removes the assumption of no uncertainty, it can be seen that most investors prefer some current payment in the form of a dividend. It is the uncertainty associated with the future financial outcomes of the firm that prompts owners to prefer some current payment as compensation for their invested capital. As current dividend payments reduce investor uncertainty, the investors discount the firm's earnings at a lower rate, thereby placing a higher value on the firm's stock. If dividends are not paid investor uncertainty will increase, raising the rate at which the firm's earnings are discounted and lowering the value of the stock. The argument with respect to the reduction of uncertainty is also closely allied to MM's argument that the value of the firm's shares may increase only because of the informational content of dividends. MM, however, do not concede that the increased stock price results from an increase in the value placed on earnings due to a reduction in the uncertainty of returns. Rather, they suggest that the increased value placed on the earnings is based only on the expectation that they will be higher in the future. The real difficulty in disproving MM's theory of the irrelevance of dividends is in countering MM's use of the clientele effect argument to suggest that the firm's shareholders are indifferent to whether they receive dividends or capital gains.

Removing MM's assumption of no taxes, it is obvious that stockholders will not be indifferent as to whether they receive dividends or capital gains since the tax rates on capital gains are lower. However, this does not necessarily disprove the clientele effect. Both the effect of taxes favouring capital gains and the uncertainty of returns must be considered by the firm establishing a dividend policy. Although the reduction of uncertainty suggests the need for dividend payments and the presence of taxes indicates an advantage of retaining earnings, both these factors suggest that the cash dividend decision is an important one and that dividends are relevant.

Modigliani and Miller use the assumption of no flotation or brokerage costs and no taxes to argue that if the internal investment opportunities of the firm are greater than the firm's cost of equity funds it should retain all its earnings, since, if the earnings were paid out as dividends, the recipients would use the dividends to purchase added shares of the firm's stock. Since the firm would not have to pay any flotation costs and the stockholders would have to pay neither brokerage costs nor taxes, their proportion of the firm's equity would be no different than if the firm had retained the earnings. This argument, like the other arguments presented by Modigliani and Miller, is valid only given their highly restrictive and unrealistic assumptions.

The dividend relevance school suggests instead that stockholders do have a preference for current dividends — that, in fact, there is a direct relationship between the dividend policy of the firm and its market value. It is argued that investors are generally risk averters and attach less risk to current as opposed to future dividends or capital gains. The 'bird-in-hand' argument suggests that a firm's dividend policy is relevant since investors prefer some dividends now in order to reduce their uncertainty. When investors are less uncertain about their returns, they discount the firm's earnings at a lower rate — therefore placing a higher value on the firm.

OPTIMUM DIVIDEND POLICY

Accepting that there is an optimum dividend policy, it is then necessary to find an approach to decide what the pay-out ratio should be. One approach would be to assess the net preference for dividends over capital gains; this is illustrated by curve A in Figure 1. This curve shows how the share price is likely to vary with the size of pay-out ratio.

Curve B shows the effect of higher pay-out ratios in reducing share values. This reduction of share values is due to the fact that higher pay-out ratios require that outside funds be obtained to replace the dividends paid.

Curve C shows the combined influences of these two factors on share prices.

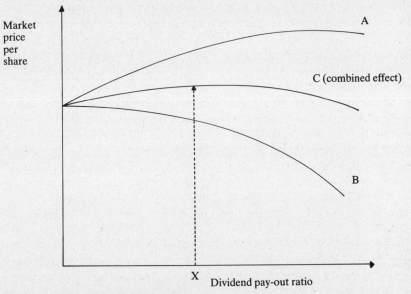

Figure 1　Optimum dividend policy

If the company does not have sufficient investments to use up all its earnings, the residue should be earmarked for payment as dividends.

Another approach which may be adopted has been propounded by E. M. Lerner and W. T. Carleton 'Integration of capital budgeting and stock valuation' *American Economic Review*, September 1964. They suggested that equity values are determined by two factors:

(a) Demand for funds: the greater the amount of funds retained, the lower will be the marginal rate of return.

(b) The supply of funds: the cost of equity is assumed to be dependent on dividend and growth expectations, which in turn depend on the rate of earnings retention. It was argued that when a company selects a retention rate, it is effectively committing itself to providing a given return on investment. As the earnings retention rate increases firms are committed to providing a higher return but the return from marginal investments is declining.

The optimum dividend pay-out ratio can be assessed as the point at which further retentions would be unjustified, because the higher return required by investors could not be met by the marginal return from extra investments.

10   Finance for overseas trade and foreign exchange management

INTERNATIONAL MONEY MARKETS

A company is not confined to raising finance on the domestic money markets but can obtain finance on a long- or short-term basis on the international money markets. Two major sources of loans for a UK exporter are Eurocurrency and Eurobonds.

EUROCURRENCY

The Eurocurrency market is the short- to medium-term end of the Euromarkets and is by far the largest of the international financial markets. It consists of banks that accept deposits and make loans in foreign currencies. Although the Eurocurrency market is closely tied to the foreign exchange market, the two markets are quite distinct in function. In the foreign exchange market, one currency is exchanged for another; in the Eurocurrency market deposits are accepted and loans are granted more often than not in the same currency.

The function of external financial intermediation is performed by specific financial institutions, usually referred to as Eurobanks. A Eurobank can be defined as 'a financial intermediary that simultaneously bids for time deposits and makes loans in a currency, or currencies, other than that of the country in which it is located'.

The important distinction between the external and domestic financial markets lies not in the overt nature of deposits and loans, but rather in the fact that Eurocurrency banking is not subject to domestic banking regulation, such as reserve requirements and interest rate restrictions. This enables Eurobanks to operate more efficiently, cheaply and competitively than their domestic counterparts and to attract intermediation business out of the domestic and into the external money market. Thus the market only operates in those currencies, such as the US dollar and German mark, that are relatively freely convertible into other currencies, and Eurobanks are located only in those countries that refrain from regulating foreign currency banking activities. It can be noted that most bank deposits of currency outside the country of the currency's origin are in US dollars and so the term 'Eurodollars' is occasionally used to describe all Eurocurrencies.

The absence of reserve requirements and regulation enables Eurobanks to offer slightly better terms to both borrowers and lenders. Therefore Eurodollar deposit rates are somewhat higher, and effective lending rates a little lower, than they are in the US money markets.

Eurocurrency lending

Eurocurrency loans are short-term loans. The term of a loan may be as long as five years, but most lending is for three months or less. There are a number of types of loan available:

(a) *Fixed interest loans*   These will usually be medium-term loans of up to five years. The borrower knows in advance what his interest payments will be, but the vulnerability of market interest rates on the market is likely to place a limit on the amount and duration of fixed interest lending which banks are prepared to allow.

(b) *Roll-over loans*   Most Eurocurrency loans to bank customers are roll-over loans. These are loans whereby the bank agrees to provide finance to the borrower for a given period of time, e.g., five years, but the interest rate on the loan is subject to renegotiation at pre-arranged intervals of every three or six months.

(c) *Stand-by credits*   A stand-by credit is an overdraft facility offered by a bank to a customer in a Eurocurrency. The cost of borrowing will be at an agreed rate or according to an agreed formula. In addition the bank will charge a commitment fee of about 1% for funds made available to the customer under the credit but which he then fails to draw.

(d) *Syndicated credits or loans*   These are large Eurocurrency loans put together for a single customer by a syndicate of banks, usually for a longer term than the Eurocurrency loans described above.

Participants in Eurocurrency markets

The participants in the Eurocurrency markets are diverse in character. Hundreds of banks and corporations, mostly originating in North America, Western Europe and Japan, are regular borrowers and depositors in the market. Commercial banks form the institutional core of the market. The banks enter the Eurodollar market both as depositors and lenders; they purchase as well as issue financial securities. The 20 or so of the world's biggest banks play a dominant role in the Eurodollar market.

The bulk of the private non-bank participants continues to be firms engaged in international business as exporters, importers, investors, and those with internationally diversified manufacturing operations. They are attracted by the size of the market. While in national markets there is invariably credit rationing during periods of tight credit, often mandated by government, in the Euromarkets the funds are always available for those able and willing to pay the price. Equally important, the market's size assures that the marginal cost of funds is less.

A second advantage to international firms is that the funds raised in the international money market have no restrictions as to where they can be deployed once lenders have been satisfied that the intended purpose will not jeopardise the prospects for servicing the loan(s).

Growth of Eurocurrency markets

The introduction of convertibility between currencies in the major western European countries from 1958 made it easier to transfer funds between financial centres and so to hold Eurocurrency deposits.

We can identify a number of reasons explaining the growth in the Eurocurrency markets:

(a) Favourable interest rates can be obtained by both borrowers and depositors.

(b) International companies have grown in size and find it useful to hold cash balances in a variety of currencies, especially US dollars.

(c) Convenience for the depositor and/or borrower has contributed to the growth of the Eurocurrency markets. If a company does hold foreign currencies in bank deposits, it will still prefer to bank with a local bank in its country of operations, i.e., the desire to hold foreign currencies but still bank with a 'local' bank explains the growth of Eurocurrency deposits.

(d) Another reason why companies might want to hold foreign currency deposits when they make regular payments in those currencies is that they would avoid the transaction costs of buying and selling the currencies on the foreign exchange market and maintain exchange cover, thus avoiding the risk of adverse exchange rate movements adding to their costs.

(e) There must be a free flow of currency deposits between countries. The prominence of the Eurodollar in the markets is due not only to the importance of the dollar in world trade, but also to the fact that the US authorities have not restricted US dollar holdings by overseas residents, nor the transfer of dollar funds abroad by US residents.

(f) In the late 1950s and early 1960s some impetus to the creation of Eurocurrency markets was given by Soviet bloc countries which deposited their US dollar holdings with the European banks for fear of US government action to block their assets if they were deposited with banks in the USA.

EUROBONDS

In a fundamental sense this market performs the same function as is performed by the external money market. Funds are gathered internationally, denominated in a variety of currencies, and made available to borrowers from various countries largely without being influenced, allocated, or regulated by national authorities.

Eurobonds are quite distinct from Eurodollars, since bond markets enable investors to hold the securities issued by final borrowers directly, whereas financial intermediaries in the Eurodollar markets allow investors to hold short-term claims on Eurobanks who 'transform' deposits into long-term, riskier loans to final borrowers. In other words, the function and mechanism of the Eurobond market is quite different from that of a money market. In the Eurobond market, no intermediaries intervene between borrower and lender, although the placement of the bonds is undertaken by banks and other financial institutions in Europe and elsewhere.

Traditional foreign bonds are issued in a particular country by a foreign borrower, in the currency of that country. The Eurobond market, in contrast, is 'external'; like the Eurodollar market, it is not tied to any particular location and thereby, to a certain extent, escapes the norms and regulations that constrain individual national markets.

Eurobonds themselves are direct claims on corporations or governments and therefore are in most respects very much like domestic bonds. Their distinctiveness arises from four features:

(a) The issuing technique for Eurobonds takes the form of 'placing' rather than formal issuing, to avoid national regulations on new issues.

(b) Eurobonds are placed simultaneously in many countries through multinational syndicates of underwriting banks, who sell them to an investment clientele throughout the world.

(c) Eurobonds are sold principally in countries other than the country of issue.

(d) The interest on Eurobonds is not subject to withholding tax, which is an advantage over domestic bonds owned by non-residents, on which withholding tax is usually charged before interest is paid.

As in the Eurodollar market, interest rates on Eurobonds are closely tied to those prevailing in the domestic market, unless exchange controls or other factors inhibit arbitrage.

The external bond market, like the external money market, exists to avoid the regulation, control and allocational influence of national authorities. Again as with the Eurocurrency market, however, its existence depends on the willingness (and ability) of governments to allow investors and borrowers to move funds out of and into countries. As long as these conditions remain, and as long as governments continue to restrict or influence domestic money and capital markets, the sophisticated institutional framework that both markets have developed gives one reason to believe the Euromarkets will retain their important role in financing the growth of the world economy.

A Eurobond issue is arranged as follows:

(a) The borrower will appoint a bank to manage the bond issue. This managing bank will probably be a merchant bank or an investment bank.

(b) This managing bank invites one or more other banks or financial institutions to co-manage the issue.

(c) The managing banks try to ensure the success of the bond issue by inviting a group of banks and other financial institutions to underwrite the issue.

(d) Once the issue is underwritten, the managing banks will try to place the issue with a number of selling banks and other financial institutions.

(e) The selling banks will in turn try to place all or some of their allotment with clients. The 'placing power' of the selling banks will be a vital factor in the successful launch of a new issue, i.e., it is crucial that the selling banks should be able to place the bonds with buyers. To help the selling process, a 'prospectus' will be issued giving information about the terms and conditions of the bond, the name and details of the issuer, the purpose of the loan and selling information.

(f) Eurobond issues in the UK are usually constituted under a trust deed. The bank which is responsible for making payments to the bondholders will act as their trustee.

The interest rate on a bond issue may be fixed or variable.

EXPORT CREDIT INSURANCE

The Export Credits Guarantee Department (ECGD) was set up as long ago as 1919, and is an independent government department. Its main function is to encourage exports by providing export credit insurance to UK exporters, but in addition it provides some insurance against loss on overseas investments. ECGD's aim is to operate its insurance business at no cost to the government, and the premiums charged are expected to be sufficient to meet the cost of claims.

ECGD is also a medium for providing subsidised finance for medium-term credit. The government agrees a fixed rate of interest at which the banks will provide the neessary finance — a rate which is intended to be in accordance with international agreements — and ECGD reimburses the banks for the difference between this fixed rate and an agreed commercial rate of return. The terms offered by different suppliers are a major consideration in the award of export contracts, and the government has taken the view that subsidies to exports are justifiable in the light of the competition faced. Export credit insurance is often required by firms, both to limit their own exposure to loss and because the banks which advance the necessary finance require insurance as part of the security for their loans.

In attempting to cover its costs ECGD behaves in a similar fashion to other insurance organisations. It insists on a spread of business — it does not permit a company to insure only its more dubious risks — and it operates limits on the total credit granted to particular countries to avoid undue exposure to political risks. Insurance against the straightforward commercial risks could in principle be provided by the private insurance market, but political risks are generally too concentrated and unpredictable for private insurance.

Up to about 80% of the value of the export contract is guaranteed and ECGD normally has the right of recourse.

The guarantee for finance for exports on short-term credit is primarily the Comprehensive Bank Guarantee (bills and notes). This provides security for the exporter conducting business by means of the bill or the promissory note for contracts on terms of less than two years. The Comprehensive Bank Guarantee (open account) provides security to the borrower selling on open account and cash against documents with credit up to 180 days.

When finance is required for exports sold on medium- and long-term supplier credit, ECGD provides the Specific Bank Guarantee when existing cover is not sufficient to raise the funds. It is available only where the credit terms are two years or more and where payment is secured by bills or notes. For exporters who make considerable use of the Supplemental Extended Terms Guarantee, the Comprehensive Extended Terms Bank Guarantee is available in respect of contracts providing up to five years' credit.

EXPORT HOUSES

Export houses act as an important source of finance for exports. There are export merchants who operate as principals, buying goods outright and exporting them on their own account. The use of an export merchant by an exporter removes all export risks by effectively converting the transaction into a domestic one. Export agents or export managers offer payment to the manufacturer on evidence of shipment, thus giving credit in their own name to the foreign importer.

EXPORT FACTORING

Export factoring is designed to overcome some of the problems faced by exporters selling goods to a range of foreign customers on open account credit of up to six months. The services include immediate finance against export sales, a sales ledger accounting service in all major currencies, credit assessment service, and 100% credit cover for all approved sales. Protection against both foreign exchange and political risks is also provided, together with local payment facilities for all foreign buyers in all principal international markets. The cost of such an export factoring service is about 1-2% of gross sales.

ACCEPTANCE CREDITS

The acceptance credit is founded on the bill of exchange. Bills of exchange are essentially post-dated cheques and act as credit instruments for the financing of trade, affording at the same time the granting of trade credit and the realising of the funds locked in trade debt.

Acceptance credits are an important and widely used source of short-term funds. For most large companies and many medium-sized companies, they constitute the next most important external source of short-term funds after bank borrowing. Acceptance credits are usually obtained by negotiating a facility with the accepting house for a stated amount, which is then made available until further notice or for a minimum period.

As they are self-liquidating, acceptance credits are usually granted on an unsecured basis, but they normally require a negative pledge, that is, the customer undertakes not to pledge his assets elsewhere without the bank's consent.

FOREIGN EXCHANGE RATES

The foreign exchange rate represents the conversion relationship between two currencies and depends on demand/supply relationships between the two currencies. The foreign exchange rate is the price of one currency in terms of another.

The foreign exchange market has three notable features — it is extremely large, it is fast moving and it is highly complex.

Foreign exchange rates fluctuate according to the demand for and supply of a currency. The demand for the domestic currency in the foreign exchange markets derives from exports of goods and services plus capital inflows, irrespective of whether payment is made in domestic or foreign currency. For example, if UK exports or capital inflows into the UK are paid for in sterling, then foreigners have to purchase pounds in foreign currency markets with their own currencies, thus giving rise to the demand for pounds. Conversely, the supply of the domestic currency in the foreign exchange markets derives from imports and capital outflows, irrespective of whether actual payment is made in domestic or foreign currency. For example, if UK imports and capital outflows from the UK are paid for in sterling, then foreigners receiving these sterling payments will exchange them for their own currencies in the foreign exchange markets, and so the supply of sterling in these markets will rise.

Exchange rates fluctuate due to a number of reasons:

(a) Differing rates of inflation: for example, if the rate of inflation in the UK is 15% per annum and that in Austria is 5%, the pound would be expected to lose value against the schilling (all other things being equal) by a factor of 1.05/1.15. If the pound was worth 29 schillings at the beginning of the year, it would only be worth $29 \times (1.05/1.15) = 26.4$ schillings at the end of the year.

(b) Interest rates and capital movements between countries: foreign investors will be willing to invest their capital in countries where high rates of return are offered.

(c) Structural changes: these refer to anything which affects the 'comparative advantage' of one country's products and costs against another's; for example, discovery of oil resources, or decline in industrial productivity.

FORWARD EXCHANGE CONTRACTS

The foreign exchange market deals on two planes: it deals in transactions for immediate delivery of currency and it deals in transactions for the future delivery of currency. Forward transactions provide a way of covering a trader's risks when he has to pay or receive payments in a certain currency three or six months ahead at a time when the rate at which his own currency will exchange into the other is moving daily. Some transactions can be undertaken up to five years ahead, but the bulk of forward turnover covers periods of one month, three months and six months.

A forward exchange contract has the following components: a quantity of commodity to be delivered, a date of delivery, a place of delivery, and a price agreed upon when the contract is sold. The buyer of a forward exchange contract is obligated to take delivery under the terms of the contract. The seller of a forward exchange contract is obligated to make delivery under the terms of the contract.

Example 14 A UK importer knows on 1 September that he must pay a foreign seller Deutschmarks 25,000 in a month's time — 1 October. If the spot rate for buying Deutschmarks on 1 September is DM 4.2 to £1, the UK importer would expect to have to pay his bank $25,000/4.2 = £5,952.38$ on 1 October if the spot rate remains the same. However, the exchange rate is likely to fluctuate. If the pound weakens so that the selling rate is 4.05 the UK importer will have to pay $25,000/4.05 = £6,172.83$; more than he would have paid on 1 September. If the pound strengthens, however, and the spot selling rate is 4.4, the cost of the DM 25,000 to the importer will be $25,000/4.4 = £5,681.81$.

By a forward exchange contract, however, the importer can minimise the risk of fluctuations in spot rates. By it he may arrange with his bank that it will sell him DM 25,000 on 1 October at a rate of, say 4.1. The UK importer can now be certain that whatever the spot rate is between Deutschmarks and sterling on 1 October he will have to pay 25,000/4.1 = £6,097.56. If the spot rate is lower than 4.1 the importer will have protected himself against a weakening of sterling and hence the greater expense of having to pay more sterling to buy the Deutschmarks. If the spot rate is higher then the importer would pay more under the forward exchange contract than he would have had to pay if he bought the Deutschmarks at the spot rate on October 1. It must be noted that if the forward exchange contract works to the importer's disadvantage he cannot just forget it and buy Deutschmarks at the spot rate — the forward exchange rate is a binding contract.

The trader/importer may take a risk and gamble on movements in the exchange rate which are advantageous to him, but the prospects of speculative gain must be weighed against a total loss of profits on a transaction if the currency rates move adversely.

The forward exchange contract carries three important benefits for the trader:

(a) He knows precisely what his cash flows will be in the future; this could be important for budgeting his firm's operations.

(b) He will know in advance the cost of his purchases from abroad. This enables him to fix his own selling prices in advance.

(c) An exporter can guarantee his profit margin on a sale by fixing in advance his sterling income.

INTERNAL TECHNIQUES FOR FOREIGN EXCHANGE MANAGEMENT

One technique is basically doing nothing. If an international firm is operating in many countries with freely floating exchange rates the international equilibrium model will apply and cash flows will not alter in real terms in the long run. Management will therefore devote itself to running the business rather than worrying about foreign exchange exposure. This technique may not be suitable if non-freely floating currencies are involved.

Another management technique is the manipulation of inter-group cash flows. 'Netting' involves the consideration of how holdings of all cash-like assets in different currencies net out across the whole group. A multinational firm can construct a payments netting matrix and minimise the number of foreign exchange transactions to be made.

Example 15

(All in £000)

Receiving subsidiary	UK	Paying subsidiary W Germany	US	Total receipts
UK	—	200	300	500
W Germany	500	—	100	600
US	400	600	—	1,000
Total payments	900	800	400	2,100

	Payment	Receipt	Net payment	Net receipt
UK	900	500	400	
W Germany	800	600	200	
US	400	1,000		600

Instead of six payments being made throughout the group only two payments need to be made. The UK can pay the US £400,000 and the West Germans can pay the US £200,000. The group will effect a saving in the costs of foreign exchange transactions as the banks will only earn their margin on two rather than six transactions.

Another internal technique is that of matching. If a company has assets denominated in a foreign currency it can match these with liabilities also in a foreign currency; thus, if the foreign currency changes in value the change in value of the assets and liabilities will cancel out. If a firm has a sizeable export market in a country it can obtain finance in that country. If operating profits are lowered in home currency terms by exchange rate movements, there will be an offsetting effect as interest payments will also be reduced in home currency terms.

This process can be used externally by matching between firms who enter into a mutually beneficial system, thus 'swapping' exposures to reduce risk.

Leading and lagging is yet another technique that involves accelerating or delaying payment of inter-group accounts. This is a method of shifting liquidity between members of the group, as well as being an exchange risk management technique. Companies may be prevented from using this technique by government regulations and there may also be tax considerations.

FOREIGN EXCHANGE SYSTEMS

Principally, we can identify two extremes of foreign exchange management:

(a) *Free floating exchange* This system of exchange 'management' is said to exist when market forces alone are allowed to determine the exchange value of currencies. Market forces = capital movements, i.e., inflows and outflows. In practice, governments are usually reluctant to leave exchange rate determination completely to private market forces because of the danger that large fluctuations in exchange rates might ensue. If large fluctuations in exchange rates are to be expected under free floating, such a system may be undesirable for international trade and payments since the uncertainty caused by price fluctuations would inhibit world trade, output and employment.

(b) *Rigidly fixed exchange rate system*   Here the exchange values of currencies are fixed in terms of some common unit such as gold, e.g., the gold standard. The essential feature of the gold standard was that each country's currency had a fixed value in terms of gold and therefore exchange rates were effectively fixed.

Between these two extremes are various alternatives, two of which have operated since the ending of the gold standard in 1931:

(a) *Managed floating*   This system enables exchange rates to be determined essentially by private market forces, but governments intervene in the foreign exchange markets to try and moderate any short-term fluctuations which may arise due to destabilising capital flows or other factors. Managed floating was adopted in the 1930s after the abandonment of the gold standard when economic conditions were severe. The experience then was that floating did not appear to be very successful since individual countries depreciated their currencies so as to gain competitive advantage over their trading rivals.

(b) *Adjustable peg system*   Here exchange rates are fixed at agreed values but revaluations and devaluations of currencies can be undertaken under certain conditions. Such a system may provide fairly stable exchange rates for the development of world trade and yet still permit some degree of adjustment via the exchange rate. This system failed largely due to a reluctance of countries to adjust exchange rates, especially those countries in surplus.

LONDON INTERNATIONAL FINANCIAL FUTURES EXCHANGE (LIFFE)

The London International Financial Futures Exchange opened in London during 1982. It is based on the successful Chicago financial futures market which started in 1976.

The existence of a financial futures market offers the investor an alternative; instead of selling his gilts, he can sell futures contracts on gilts so that any fall in the value of his gilt portfolio will be balanced by the profit on the futures contracts. The purpose of the financial futures markets is to enable companies and individuals to fix in advance interest and exchange rates whose variability might otherwise have an adverse impact upon them. The prime purpose then, is to hedge business against adverse movements in interest or exchange rates. The exchange itself provides a place where the buying and selling may be conducted and so provides a means to set prices for those transactions. The commodity being bought and sold in such a market is a 'financial future'.

A *financial future* may be defined as follows:

It is a standard contract between buyer and seller, in which the buyer has a binding obligation to buy a fixed amount, at a fixed price, on a fixed date of some underlying security. The seller has a binding obligation to provide this amount under the terms agreed.

The 'underlying security' for the financial future contract may be anything from a quantity of foreign currency to a bond or a three-month time deposit. For each class of underlying security traded, or 'contract', there is a detailed contract specification laid down by the exchange which defines precisely what is contracted to be bought or sold.

The structure of the futures exchange is surprisingly complex, as many different types of organisation are involved with different roles to play in the conduct of the business of the market.

The Exchange itself provides the physical facilities for trading and the organisational infrastructure to enable futures contracts to be struck. The Exchange is responsible for:

(a) providing premises for trading;

(b) providing communications and other ancillary equipment required by traders;

(c) selection of the member firms and ensuring that members are suitably screened on application as to their financial standing and adequacy of capital resources;

(d) establishing rules of conduct and market practice;

(e) defining contract terms;

(f) establishing procedures and systems for traders;

(g) monitoring trading activity.

The Exchange itself does not in any way handle the payments associated with the contracts struck; this role is carried out separately by the International Commodities Clearing House (ICCH), an organisation owned by the London clearing banks. Broadly speaking, the ICCH is responsible for everything that happens after the original deal has been struck on the Exchange.

11   An introduction to working capital and its management

Working capital refers to a firm's investment in short-term assets — cash, short-term securities, trade debtors and stocks. Gross working capital is defined as the firm's total current assets; net working capital is current assets minus current liabilities. As long as the firm's current assets exceed its current liabilities, it has net working capital.

Working capital management is concerned with the management of the firm's current accounts which include current assets and current liabilities. The management of working capital is one of the most important aspects of the firm's overall financial management. Efficiency in this area of financial management is necessary in order to ensure the firm's long-term success and to achieve its overall goal — the maximisation of the owners' wealth. If the financial manager cannot manage the firm's working capital efficiently, these longer-run considerations become irrelevant.

The firm's current assets should be large enough to cover its current liabilities and give a reasonable margin of safety. The goal of working capital management is to manage each of the firm's current assets and current liabilities in such a way that an acceptable level of net working capital is maintained.

THE CONCEPT OF WORKING CAPITAL

As we have noted, the firm's net working capital is calculated by subtracting its current liabilities from its current assets. Most firms must operate with some amount of net working capital; how much depends largely on the industry. Underlying the use of net working capital to measure a firm's liquidity is the belief that the greater the margin by which a firm's current assets cover its short-term obligations the better it will be able to pay its bills as they are due. This expectation is based on the belief that current assets are sources of cash receipts, while current liabilities are sources of cash disbursements. However, a problem arises because each current asset and current liability has a different degree of liquidity associated with it. Although not all a firm's current assets may be converted into cash immediately, the greater the amount of current assets held, the more likely it is that some current asset can be converted into cash in order to pay a debt that is due.

An alternative definition of net working capital is that portion of a firm's current assets financed with long-term funds. The following diagrams help to explain this alternative definition.

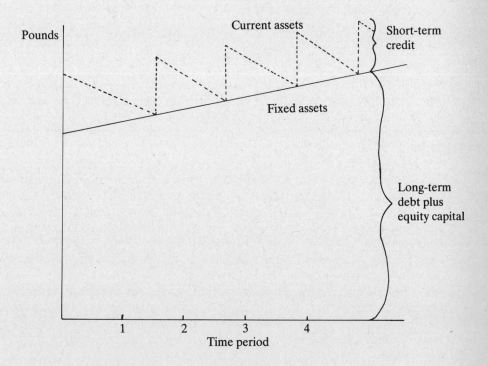

Figure 1   Fixed and current assets and their financing

Figure 1 depicts a situation in which agriculture and industry are closely related. Processors buy crops in the autumn, process them, sell the finished product and end up just before the next harvest with relatively low stocks. Short-term credit is used to finance fluctuating current assets, and fixed assets are financed with long-term funds.

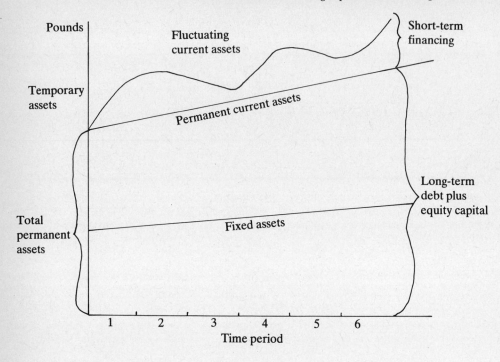

Figure 2   Financing of permanent and temporary assets

Figure 2 illustrates the traditional notion that permanent assets should be financed with long-term capital, while temporary assets should be financed with short-term credit. The distinction between permanent and temporary current assets is determined by trading conditions, e.g., a company will need to keep a minimum level of stocks to meet orders but at certain times in the year these stocks will need to be increased.

The above two situations minimise the risk that the firm may be unable to pay off its maturing obligations. For instance, suppose a firm borrows on a one-year basis and uses the funds obtained to build and equip a plant. Cash flows from the plant are not sufficient to pay off the loan at the end of the year, so the loan has to be renewed. If for some reason the lender refuses to renew the loan, then the firm has problems. Had the plant been financed with long-term debt, however, cash flows would have been sufficient to return the loan and the problem of renewal would not have arisen. Thus, if the firm finances long-term assets with permanent capital and short-term assets with temporary capital, its financial risk is lower than it would be if long-term assets were financed with short-term debt.

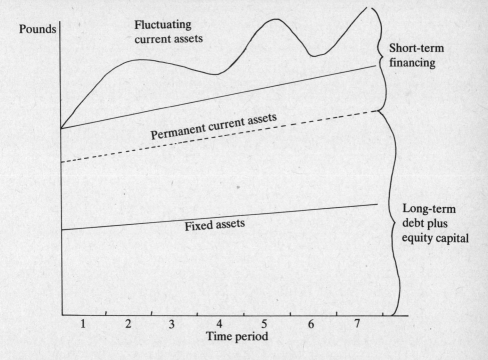

Figure 3   Split financing for permanent current assets

Figure 3 illustrates the situation for a firm that finances all its fixed assets with long-term capital but part of its permanent current assets with short-term credit.

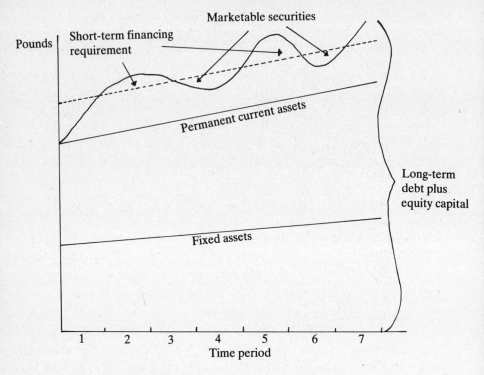

Figure 4   Seasonal demands

Figure 4 shows a situation where long-term capital is being used to meet seasonal demands. In this case, the firm uses a small amount of short-term credit to meet its peak seasonal requirements, but it also meets a part of its seasonal needs by 'storing liquidity' in the form of marketable securities during the off-season. The areas above the dashed line represent short-term financing: the areas below the dashed line represent short-term security holdings.

LONG-TERM V SHORT-TERM DEBT

There are three reasons for the use of short-term debt: flexibility, cost and risk.

(a) *Flexibility*   If the need for funds is seasonal or cyclical, the firm may not want to commit itself to long-term debt. Accordingly, if the firm expects its need for funds to diminish in the near future, or if it thinks that there is a good chance that such a reduction will occur, it may choose short-term debt for the flexibility it provides. Also, in a period of high interest rates or at a time when it is believed that interest rates are likely to fall in the near future, the financial management of a company may consider that it is useful to obtain short-term finance rather than issue long-term debentures.

(b) *Cost* The cost aspect of the maturity decision involves the term structure of interest rates or the relationship between yield and term to maturity. Although interest rates vary short-term rates are normally lower than long-term rates.

(c) *Risk* Even though short-term debt is generally less expensive than long-term debt, the use of short-term debt subjects the firm to greater risks than does long-term debt.

Since short-term debt is typically less costly than long-term debt but entails greater risk, the financial manager is faced with a trade-off between risk and rate of return.

TRADE-OFF BETWEEN PROFITABILITY AND RISK

A trade-off exists between a firm's profitability and its risk factor. Profitability, in this context, is measured by profits after expenses; a firm's profits can be increased in two ways:

(a) by increasing sales; or
(b) by decreasing costs.

Risk is measured by the probability that a firm will become technically insolvent. The risk of becoming technically insolvent is most commonly measured using either the amount of net working capital or the current ratio. In using net working capital as a measure, it is assumed that the greater the amount of net working capital a firm has, the less risky the firm is. In other words, the more net working capital, the more liquid the firm, and therefore the less likely it is to become technically insolvent. The relationship between liquidity, net working capital and risk is such that if either net working capital or liquidity increases, the firm's risk decreases and vice versa.

The nature of the trade-off

If a firm wants to increase its profitability, it must also increase its risk. If it wants to decrease risk it must decrease profitability.

(a) *Current assets* The effects of the firm's level of current assets on its profitability/risk trade-off can be illustrated using a simple ratio — the ratio of the firm's current assets to its total assets, indicating what percentage of the firm's total assets are current.

As the ratio of current assets to total assets *increases*, both the firm's profitability and its risk decrease. Its profitability decreases because current assets are less profitable than fixed assets. The risk of technical insolvency decreases because, assuming that the firm's current liabilities do not change, the increase in the firm's current assets will increase its net working capital.

A *decrease* in the ratio of current assets to total assets will result in an increase in the firm's profitability since the firm's fixed assets, which increase, generate higher returns than current assets. However, risk will also increase since the firm's net working capital will decrease with the decrease in current assets.

(b) *Current liabilities*   The effects of changing the level of a firm's current liabilities on its profitability/risk trade-off can also be demonstrated by a simple ratio —- in this case, the ratio of the firm's current liabilities to its total assets, indicating the percentage of the firm's total assets that have been financed by current liabilities.

As the ratio of current liabilities to total assets increases, the firm's profitability increases, but so does risk. A decrease in the ratio of current liabilities to total assets will, on the other hand, decrease the profitability of the firm. There will be a corresponding decrease in risk due to the decreased level of current liabilities, which will cause an increase in the firm's net working capital.

WORKING CAPITAL AND THE OPERATING CYCLE

The operating cycle is the length of time between the company's outlay on raw materials, wages and other expenditures and the inflow of cash from the sale of goods. In a manufacturing business this is the average time that raw materials remain in stock, less the period of credit taken from suppliers, plus the time taken for producing goods, plus the time the goods remain in finished inventory, plus the time taken by customers to pay for the goods. This is an important concept for the management of working capital and cash because the longer the operating cycle the more financial resources the company needs. Management needs to ensure that the cycle does not become too long. The operating cycle is illustrated in Figure 5.

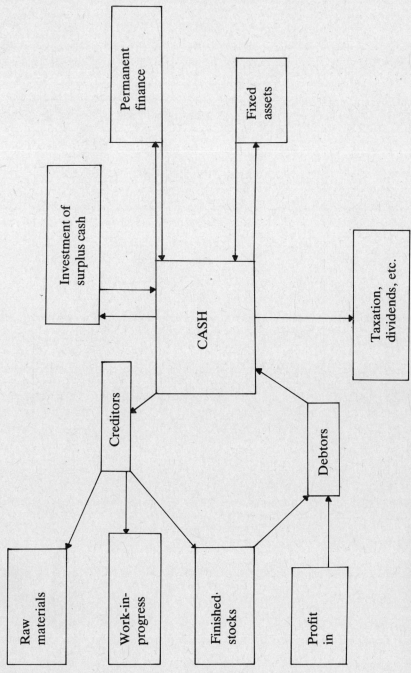

Figure 5   The operating cycle

The cycle is only the time-span between production costs and the cash returns; it says nothing in itself of the amount of working capital that will be needed over this period. Less will in fact be required at the beginning than at the end; initially, the only expenditure is on the materials, but as wages and other expenses are incurred the amount of working capital required increases over the cycle.

Short-term working capital is required to support a given level of turnover, to pay for the goods and services before the cash is received from sales. The optimum level is the amount which causes no strain on liquid resources and results in no idle cash. To determine the amount required it is necessary to know the estimated sales for the period, and the characteristics and scale of the operating cycle.

In order to make sure the cycle does not become too long and to achieve some improved synchronisation between the cash inflows and outflows, certain elements within the cash cycle can be manipulated. For example, payments to suppliers could be slowed, stocks of raw materials and finished goods could be reduced, cash sales only could be accepted and efforts could be made to speed up the production process. It must be noted, however, that in trying to shorten the cash cycle there may be detrimental effects elsewhere. For example, lowering stock levels would reduce the time they were kept prior to sale but would also increase the probability of a stock-out situation. It is often said that the shorter the cash operating cycle the greater the cash velocity within the firm — thus the more efficient is the management of the firm's working capital. In reality, however, the efficient management of working capital is more complex than this, with a trade-off required between costs and benefits which are often hard both to identify and quantify.

CASH MANAGEMENT

Controlling the investment in current assets begins with cash management. Cash consists of the firm's holdings of current and deposit accounts, with current accounts being by far the more important for most firms.

We can identify three primary motives for holding cash:

(a) *Transactions motive* The transactions motive for holding cash is to enable the firm to conduct its ordinary business, i.e., purchases and sales.

(b) *Precautionary motive* The precautionary motive relates primarily to the predictability of cash inflows and outflows. If predictability is high, less cash must be held against an emergency or any other contingency. Another factor that strongly influences the precautionary motive for holding cash is the ability to borrow cash on short notice when circumstances necessitate. Borrowing flexibility is primarily a matter of the strength of the firm's relations with banking institutions and other credit sources.

(c) *Speculative motive*   The speculative motive for holding cash is to be ready for profit-making opportunities that may arise. By and large, business accumulations of cash for speculative purposes are not widely found.

Cash budgets

Management is kept informed about the cash position of the company by the cash budget. The cash budget involves estimating the flow of funds into and out of the firm, as called for by the operating and capital plans.

It is necessary in the cash budgeting exercise to estimate expenditures. The cost of raw materials, wages, and other items will have been paid, possibly long before the product is sold. The finished goods may well have to wait in inventory before their sale. The cash budget will need to consider the production schedules to estimate the cash outflow: it is not possible to link directly the expenses with the sales. All other items affecting the cash flow must also be allowed for and shown in the budget. These include dividends and interest, tax payments and any item of a capital nature, such as purchase of new equipment or sale of old equipment.

In practice, company managers rely heavily on the ability to sell short-term investments to replenish the firm's cash balance. The availability of near cash fundamentally affects cash balance management. The company policy becomes oriented towards forecasting heavy future cash needs and purchasing securities of a maturity to match these requirements over time. Such a policy is very dependent on the accuracy of cash flow budgets. To the extent that cash flows are predictable in timing and in size, this reliance on the trading of securities to meet cash needs may be economic. If cash flows can be predicted with a reasonable degree of accuracy, the company can be more dependent on its short-term deposits and securities and needs to maintain smaller cash balances over time. The greater the uncertainty of the cash flow, the larger the cash balance that needs to be maintained, and so the greater the opportunity cost.

The cash budget is designed not only to estimate cash flows but also to provide control tools, particularly in the individual budgets for cash sales and collections, payments for inventory purchases, and employment and other cash expenses.

Need for adequate cash

Sound working capital management requires the maintenance of an adequate amount of cash for several specific reasons:

(a)   It is essential that the firm has sufficient cash to take trade discounts.

(b)   Since the credit and acid test ratios are key items in credit analysis, it is important that the firm, in order to maintain its credit standing, meets the standards of the line of business in which it is engaged. Strong credit enables the firm to purchase goods from trade suppliers on favourable terms and to maintain its line of credit with banks and other sources of credit.

(c) Cash is useful for taking advantage of favourable business opportunities that may come along from time to time.

(d) The firm should have sufficient liquidity to meet emergencies.

The goal of the financial manager in cash management is to gauge matters so finely that he never actually has more cash on hand than will be needed, because surplus cash is an idle asset and as such it incurs an opportunity cost, i.e., the cost to the company of what it could earn if invested elsewhere in securities or in longer-term deposits.

The extent to which cash is put to effective use within the business will reflect agreeably in the profit levels, but there are limits. The loss of liquidity due to maintaining very low cash balances and not having overdraft arrangements could lead the company into difficulties. Slowness in paying debts may mean that cash discounts are forfeited, or, perhaps more seriously, that suppliers are lost. The key to management of cash and of all working capital is, therefore, a matter of striking a balance between risk and profitability.

Setting cash balances

In setting cash balances for itself a company can use ratio analysis. One measure that would assist in the management of cash is the ratio of the cash balance to the level of current assets:

$$\text{Cash proportion ratio} = \frac{\text{Cash balance}}{\text{Current assets}}$$

The financial management of a company could benefit from a study of the movement over time of the cash to current asset ratio.

Another approach to determining the amount of cash that a company may need to carry is to examine the cash balance in relation to the sales of the period. This can be done by studying the inventory/turnover ratio:

$$\text{Cash turnover} = \frac{\text{Sales per period}}{\text{Initial cash balance}}$$

The success of working capital management and cash management also depends upon knowledge of the cash flow position of the company. The finance manager should know his company's current cash position and its expected cash position at various times in the future. To do this, he will need to estimate the company's cash needs, its ability to finance them, the possible sources from which any shortfall can be financed, and what to do with any surplus cash.

Cash forecasting

The cash forecast is used to identify two distinct situations: future cash shortages and future cash surpluses.

In terms of cash shortages, the cash forecast should be able to identify the expected magnitude and duration of such events so that the company's management can arrange for the appropriate remedial action to be taken in good time.

In terms of cash surpluses, the cash forecast would need to make a distinction between a temporary surplus and a more persistent surplus. In the former case arrangements can be made to invest the cash in short-term deposits, whilst in the latter case a strategic decision would be necessary on whether dividend payments should be substantially increased over time to eradicate the surplus or to expand substantially the company's operations to absorb spare cash into productive investment opportunities.

Cash forecasting can be approached by means of the balance sheet ratio, but also by adopting a funds flow technique, i.e., 'receipts' and 'payments'.

WORKING CAPITAL AND THE FUNDS FLOW STATEMENT

A funds flow statement can take one of two forms. One is an historical document showing what has happened in the past, where the funds have come from and where they have been used. The second type of funds statement is a tool for financial management, for financial planning. The former relates to the past, the latter to the future. The statements will disclose the extent to which long-term funds have been used or are to be used to finance working capital needs or vice versa. It will show whether the purchase of long-term assets has been or will be financed with short-term funds. It will show the movement of funds within the working capital items and whether working capital in total is being increased or decreased.

A funds flow statement does not go into detail concerning the movement of cash, it is more interested in where the funds are coming from over the next few years and how they are to be used. It is necessary to estimate the funds that will be retained in the business each year. The need for funds will depend upon capital investment plans and working capital needs.

The funds flow statement shows the sources of funds of the company, and the way in which these funds have been used. (Note: funds are not cash!) For example, it is possible to take over another company and to pay for this by issuing shares or debentures to the selling shareholders. There is no cash involved and so this transaction would not appear in a cash flow statement, but it would appear in a funds flow statement.

It is necessary for a funds flow statement to distinguish between the movement in long-term and short-term assets and liabilities. It is also necessary to distinguish between the use of funds for the purchase of fixed assets and the use of funds to finance increases in working capital.

There are two further important types of current asset (apart from cash) which form part of a company's working capital:

(a) inventory;
(b) accounts receivable — including trade credit and consumer credit.

Stock.

INVENTORY MANAGEMENT

The cost of holding inventory includes not only storage cost and the risk of spoilage or obsolescence, but also the opportunity cost of capital. The benefits of holding inventory are often indirect. For example, a large inventory of finished goods reduces the chances of a 'stock-out' if demand is unexpectedly high. Bulk orders for raw materials, although they lead to large average inventories, may be worth while if the firm can obtain lower prices from suppliers. A large inventory of finished goods allows longer, more economical production runs.

The task of inventory management is to assess these benefits and costs and to strike a sensible balance.

Types of inventory

There are three basic types of inventory:

(a) *Raw materials* The raw materials inventory contains items purchased by the firm — usually basic materials. All manufacturing firms have a raw materials inventory of some kind. The actual level of each raw material maintained depends on the lead time it takes to receive orders, the frequency of use, the amount of investment required and the physical characteristics of inventory. The lead time must be considered, since, if the production process is to operate smoothly, the firm must always have enough raw materials on hand to supply production demands. The frequency of use of inventory also affects the level maintained. The inventory of frequently used raw materials will generally be higher than the inventory of raw materials that are used relatively infrequently. In addition the dollar investment required to maintain a given level of inventory must be considered. The physical characteristics of raw materials also affect the level of inventory. For example, a cheap item with a long lead time before orders are received but a short shelf-life would not be ordered in large quantities since, if it were, a portion of the inventory would be likely to spoil or deteriorate before it was used in the production process.

(b) *Work-in-process* The work-in-process inventory consists of all items currently being used in the production process.

A direct relationship exists between the length of the firm's production process and its average level of work-in-process inventory. In other words, the longer the firm's production cycle, the higher the level of work-in-process inventory expected. A higher work-in-process inventory results in higher costs since the firm's money is tied up for a longer period of time. The firm should try to minimise the length of the inventory cycle whilst keeping stock-outs to a minimum. Efficient management of the production process should reduce the work-in-process inventory, which should speed the inventory turnover and reduce the firm's operating cash requirement.

(c) *Finished goods* The finished goods inventory consists of items that have been produced but not yet sold. Some manufacturing firms that produce to order carry very low finished goods inventories since virtually all items are sold before they are produced. With general manufacturing firms producing and selling a diversified group of products, however, most merchandise is produced in anticipation of sales. The level of finished goods is largely dictated by projected sales demand, the production process, and the investment in finished goods required.

Debtors

ACCOUNTS RECEIVABLE MANAGEMENT

Accounts receivable represent the extension of credit on an open account by the firm to its customers. In order to keep current customers and attract new ones, most manufacturing concerns find it necessary to offer credit.

Credit policy

A firm's credit policy provides the guidelines for determining whether to extend credit to a customer and how much credit to extend.

Credit standards

The firm's credit standards define the minimum criteria for the extension of credit to a customer. There are a number of key variables according to which credit standards may be determined:

(a) *Clerical expenses* A relaxation of credit standards will increase clerical costs as a larger credit department will be required to service the added accounts, whilst a tightening of credit standards should decrease clerical costs.

(b) *Investment in receivables* There is a cost associated with carrying accounts receivable. The higher a firm's average accounts receivable are, the more expensive they are to carry, and vice versa. If the firm relaxes its credit standards, the average level of accounts receivable should rise, whereas tightening the firm's credit standards should decrease the average level of accounts receivable.

(c) *Bad debt expenses* Another variable affected by changes in credit standards is bad debt expenses. The risk of acquiring a bad debt increases as credit standards are relaxed and decreases as credit standards become more restrictive.

(d) *Sales volume* As credit standards relax sales volume increases.

In order to decide whether the firm should relax its credit standards, the additional profit contribution from sales must be compared to the cost of the marginal investment in accounts receivable. If the additional profit contribution is greater than marginal costs, the credit standards should be relaxed; otherwise the current credit standards should remain unchanged.

Cash discounts

Cash discounts are offered by the seller to the buyer to encourage early payment before the end of a period of credit. Whether the buyer decides to pay early and takes advantage of the cash discount depends to some extent on the size of the discount. The discount usually must be quite substantial if it is to encourage early payment; it is therefore an expense for the seller and consequently should only be used by firms when cash is needed and is in short supply.

The use of cash discounts in the UK has, in fact, declined in recent years. This is largely because of the practice of some purchasers in taking discounts, whether or not they have paid within the specified time. If this happens it is very difficult for the supplier to try to obtain the amount which has incorrectly been taken as a discount. As a result many suppliers have abandoned cash discounts. The decline in cash discounts is also due to the fact that it is increasingly apparent to suppliers that cash discounts do not improve turnover.

In place of cash discounts, quantity discounts are now more often offered. In P. R. A. Kirkman's survey in *Modern Credit Management* (1977) of the credit management practices of *The Times 1000* leading UK companies, two-thirds of respondents offered quantity discounts. Such discounts allow buyers of large quantities to obtain reductions in the unit price of the goods they buy.

Debt collection

A number of different collection techniques are typically employed but they usually have the following format:

(a) Letters: a reminder is sent to the customer of his/her obligation. If the account is not paid within a certain period of time after the letter has been sent, a second more demanding letter is sent.

(b) Telephone calls: If letters prove unsuccessful, the company's credit manager may call the customer and personally request immediate payment.

(c) Personal visits.

(d) Employment of collection agencies.

(e) Legal action.

RELATIONSHIP BETWEEN INVENTORY AND ACCOUNTS RECEIVABLE

The level and the management of inventory and accounts receivable are closely related. Generally, in the case of manufacturing firms, when an item is sold it moves from inventory to accounts receivable and ultimately to cash. Due to the close relationship between these current assets, the inventory management and accounts receivable management functions should not be viewed independently of each other. For example, the decision to extend credit to a customer can result in an increased level of sales, which can be supported only by higher levels of inventory and accounts receivable. The credit terms extended will also have an impact on the investment in inventory and receivables, since longer credit terms may allow a firm to move items from inventory to accounts receivable.

12   Portfolio theory and capital asset pricing

A portfolio is simply a collection or group of securities considered in total as a single investment unit. A portfolio can be defined very broadly and be taken to include property, antiques, works of art, bullion and commodities, as well as financial securities. When any particular portfolio is assessed, the concern will be with its overall characteristics, its expected return and its risk.

Portfolio theory is concerned with the problem of making a selection of optimum investments in respect of a particular investor, taking into account the anticipated returns and the risks associated with them, and the requirements of the investor in the short, medium and long term and his attitude towards risk. Most approaches to portfolio theory incorporate some statistical measure of the risks involved. An efficient portfolio is one such that no other portfolio exists which offers the same return with lower risk, or the same risk with higher return. A main innovator in respect of portfolio theory was Markowitz, who applied statistical techniques to the assessment of risk.

DIVERSIFICATION AND RISK

It is of course true that as a rule a person will not enter on a risky business, unless, other things being equal, he expects to gain from it more than he would in other trades open to him, after his probable losses had been deducted from his probable gains on a fair actuarial estimate. [Alfred Marshall *Industry and Trade,* Macmillan, 1921.]

Alfred Marshall was writing in the late nineteenth early twentieth century and therefore this statement shows that the idea of risk diversification (i.e., 'not putting all of one's eggs into one basket') is by no means a recent one. What is more recent is the provision of a formal theoretical framework in which both the analysis of the benefits of risk diversification and the choice of a particular portfolio can be made on a 'scientific' basis. This development, as we have noted, stemmed largely from the work of Harry Markowitz.

The theory developed by Markowitz made a number of crucial assumptions with respect to both the behaviour of investors and the nature of their analysis of the potential returns available on portfolio securities:

(a) Investors are assumed to be concerned with maximising the expected utility of their portfolio of securities over the single period under consideration.

(b) Investors are assumed to have beliefs about the potential returns available on individual securities in the form of subjective probability distributions of expected returns. It is also assumed that investors have an estimate of the covariability of the expected returns on the securities available.

(c) It follows that, when combinations of securities are chosen to form various portfolios, these portfolios can be completely described, from the investor's point of view, by the mean and variance of their expected returns.

(d) Investors have utility functions of a type which enables them to choose portfolios solely on the basis of their estimated risk and expected return, and that in this choice the investors display risk aversion. From this it follows that, at a given level of risk, investors prefer more returns to less, and that at a given level of return they prefer less risk to more.

Portfolio risk for companies

The firm should be viewed as having a portfolio of projects selected in a fashion consistent with the goal of maximisation of shareholder wealth. (We will consider the theory of portfolio selection later in the chapter.) New capital budgeting proposals must be considered in the light of both existing projects and other proposed projects, and the projects selected must be those that best diversify, or reduce, the firm's risk while generating an acceptable return. Successful diversification may make the risk of a group, or portfolio, of projects less than the sum of the risk of the individual projects.

Correlation of projects

In order to diversify risk for the creation of an efficient portfolio (one that allows the firm to achieve the maximum return for a given level of risk or to minimise risk for a given level of return), the concept of correlation must be understood. Correlation is a statistical measure that indicates the relationship, if any, between series of numbers representing anything from cash flows to test data. If the two series move together, they are positively correlated; if the series move in opposite directions, they are negatively correlated. The existence of perfectly correlated — especially negatively correlated — projects is quite rare.

In order to diversify project risk and thereby reduce the firm's overall risk, the projects that are best combined or added to the existing portfolio of projects are those that have a negative (or low positive) correlation with existing projects. By combining negatively correlated projects, the overall variability of returns or risk can be reduced. Figure 1 illustrates the result of diversifying to reduce risk.

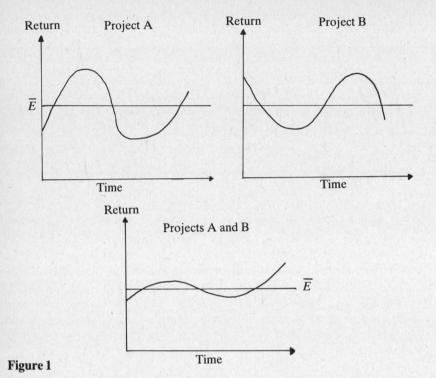

Figure 1

It shows that a portfolio containing the negatively correlated projects A and B, both having the same expected return, $\bar{E}$, also has the return $\bar{E}$, but less risk (i.e., less variability of return) than either of the projects taken separately. This type of risk is sometimes described as diversifiable or alpha risk; this topic is returned to at the end of the chapter.

The creation of a portfolio by combining two perfectly correlated projects cannot reduce the portfolio's overall risk below the risk of the least risky project, while the creation of a portfolio combining two projects that are perfectly negatively correlated can reduce the portfolio's total risk to a level below that of either of the component projects, which in certain situations may be zero. Combining projects with correlations falling between perfect positive correlation (i.e., a correlation coefficient of +1) and perfect negative correlation (i.e., a correlation coefficient of −1), can therefore reduce the overall risk of a portfolio.

Measurement of portfolio risk

In order to measure risk in investment analysis, we may express estimates of the results of a project as probability distributions, by giving a list of the possible cash flows with an estimate of the relative likelihood (probability) of the occurrence of each one. This leads to a characterisation of the results of a project in two measures:

(a) the expected value: the weighted average of the present values of the various possible outcomes, using probabilities as weights; and,
(b) a measure of the dispersion of possible outcomes (the risk of the project), conveniently summarised in a statistical quantity, the variance or standard deviation.

Benefits of diversification

The gains in risk reduction from portfolio diversification depend inversely upon the extent to which the returns on securities in a portfolio are positively correlated. Ideally the securities should display negative correlation. This implies that if a pair of securities has a negative correlation of returns, then in circumstances where one of the securities is performing badly the other is likely to be doing well, and vice versa in reverse circumstances. Therefore the 'average' return on holding the two securities is likely to be much 'safer' than investing in one of them alone.

Portfolio analysis

This analysis starts from the argument that investors are able to hold a portfolio of investments and that it is the effect on the aggregate risk of the whole portfolio that is important in decisions about particular activities. The analysis leads to the conclusion that the risk of a project, considered independently, is relatively unimportant because part of that risk can be diversified away when the project is combined with others. A project may have a high level of risk in itself and yet be a good hedge — it may be expected to show high returns if circumstances prevail in which other investments have low returns and vice versa. In such circumstances the separate risk of the project would be no deterrent to its acceptance; rather, it would normally be seen as a highly desirable investment. Such a project may be said to have a low relative risk. Another investment, having a high level of risk in itself may tend to have returns which are positively associated with returns from other investments; it may have high returns when other investments have high returns and low returns when they have low returns. The risk of such a project *is* an independent consideration; it cannot be diversified away by adjustments to the portfolio. An investment with returns which are positively associated with the returns on other investments may be said to have high relative risk.

The 'efficient' selection of portfolios

Earlier in the chapter we considered the assumptions behind Markowitz's theory of investor behaviour when analysing the potential returns. The theory assumes that they choose portfolios on the basis of the mean and variance of their expected returns and furthermore that they are rational and display risk aversion. These assumptions imply that investors will only consider investing in what Markowitz termed 'efficient' portfolios, that is, portfolios which promise the greatest expected return for the estimated levels of risk. In general, risk aversion implies that the rational investor will want to take on as much expected return as possible and minimise the amount of risk in his portfolio.

It is possible to combine two securities to form a number of portfolios offering various levels of risk and, by implication, various levels of expected return. The same principle holds for portfolios, and as any two existing portfolios could be combined to form a number of other portfolios, the continuing assumptions of infinite security and portfolio divisibility suggest that a dominating 'efficient set' of portfolios could be generated. This is shown in Figure 2.

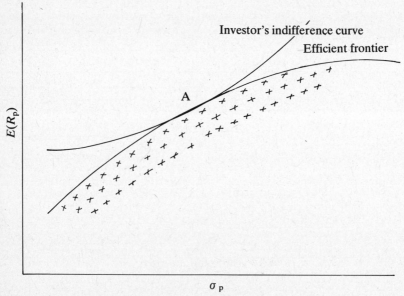

Figure 2   The efficient frontier and portfolio selection

In this figure the curve marked 'efficient frontier' traces the locus of the combinations of risk/return on all available efficient portfolios. Portfolios on the curve obviously dominate the risk/return combinations available on portfolios and securities to the right of it. Portfolios offering risk/return further to the left of the efficient frontier would be preferred, if available, but the investor's estimations of the risk/return characteristics of currently available portfolios suggests that these are currently unattainable. The efficient frontier marks the optimum set of portfolios available to the investor. His optimum portfolio, indicated by the point at which he chooses to locate himself on the efficient frontier, will depend upon his relative aversion to risk.

Risk-free securities and their effect on portfolio selection

The portfolios represented by the crosses on the graph in Figure 2 are assumed to be made up of investments involving some risk. Although it is possible to reduce the risk of a portfolio by suitable diversification, it may not be possible to eliminate it altogether. Let us consider the effect on the portfolio selection of including in our analysis a risk-free security which might, for example, be a government stock.

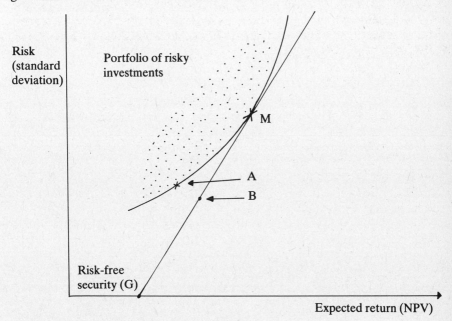

Figure 3   Inclusion of a risk-free security

Figure 3 shows a tangent to the efficient frontier drawn through the value of return yielded by the risk-free security. Points on this line can be considered as representing portfolios consisting partly of portfolio M and partly of the risk-free security, G. This can be seen by, for example, considering A and B. A is a portfolio of risky investments with the same return as B but with a higher risk. B is obviously preferable.

CAPITAL ASSET PRICING MODEL

The capital asset pricing model (CAPM) was developed primarily to explain the behaviour of security prices and provide a mechanism whereby investors could readily assess the impact of a proposed security investment on their overall portfolio risk and return. Although the theory cannot be readily applied to the internal capital budgeting/project selection process, it does provide useful insights into the nature of the risk-return trade-offs considered to be part of the capital budgeting process.

The CAPM is expressed by the following formula:

$$(R_s - i) = \beta (R_m - i)$$

where R_s = expected return from the particular security
i = risk-free rate of return
R_m = expected return from the market portfolio
β = the beta coefficient for the particular security

This can be reorganised to give:

$$R_s = i + \beta (R_m - i)$$

Assumptions

The CAPM relies on a number of assumptions that create a nearly perfect world in which the model can be most clearly defined. Although they appear to be unrealistic, empirical studies have confirmed their reasonableness and have provided support for the existence of the relationships described by CAPM. The basic assumptions are related to the efficiency of the markets and investor preferences.

(a) *Efficient markets* The market-place in which investors make transactions in securities is assumed to be highly efficient. This means that investors all have the same information with respect to securities and that this information is accurate. All investors are assumed to view securities in the light of a common ownership period, usually one year. There are no restrictions on investment, no taxes, and no transactions costs.

(b) *Investor preferences* Investors are presumed to prefer to earn higher, rather than lower, returns; at the same time they are averse to risk, preferring lower, rather than higher, risk.

Types of risk

A security risk is said to consist of two components:

(a) *Unsystematic risk* This is sometimes referred to as 'diversifiable risk'. It represents the portion of an asset's risk that can be eliminated through diversification. It results from the occurrence of uncontrollable or random events, e.g., strikes.

(b) *Systematic risk* This is also called non-diversifiable risk. It is attributed to forces that affect all firms and are therefore not unique to the given firm — factors such as war, inflation, etc. This risk can be assessed relative to the risk of a diversified portfolio of securities, which is commonly referred to as the market portfolio or the market.

Any investor can create a portfolio of assets that will diversify away all diversifiable risk and therefore the only relevant risk is the systematic or non-diversifiable risk. Any investor must thus be concerned solely with the non-diversifiable risk, which reflects the contribution of an asset to the risk of the portfolio. The risk is not the same for each asset, but rather different assets will affect the portfolio differently. As the relevant risk differs from asset to asset, its measurement is important in order to allow investors to select assets offering the desired risk/return characteristics to be included in their portfolios. The CAPM provides a mechanism that can be used to relate risk and return.

The beta coefficient of a market portfolio

In order to assess an asset's non-diversifiable risk, its beta coefficient must be determined. This can be found by examining an asset's historic returns relative to the returns of the market (i.e., market portfolio). The beta coefficient can be viewed as an index of the degree of responsiveness of the asset return to the market return.

As the market portfolio represents all shares on the stock market, it follows that the beta coefficient of the market portfolio must be 1, and all other betas are viewed relative to this value. Thus, if the return from the market portfolio rises by, say, 2%, the coefficient would be:

$$\frac{\text{Increase in return on investment (which is in this case) market portfolio}}{\text{Increase in return on market portfolio}} = \frac{2\%}{2\%} = 1$$

The beta factor of a market portfolio

If the return from the market portfolio rises or falls, we should expect a corresponding rise or fall in the return from an individual share. The amount of this corresponding rise or fall depends on the beta factor of the share. The beta factor of an investor's portfolio is the total of the weighted average beta factors of each security in the portfolio.

Example   If an investor holds a portfolio consisting of:

Security	Percentage of portfolio	Beta factor of security	Weighted average
Hanson Trust	20%	0.90	0.180
ICI	10%	1.25	0.125
Cadbury's	15%	1.10	0.165
RTZ	20%	1.15	0.230
British Petroleum	35%	0.70	0.245
	100%		0.945

The beta factor of this portfolio would be 0.945

Holding a portfolio with a beta factor of 0.945 is equivalent to an investor holding 94.5% of his investment in the average market portfolio and 5.5% of his investment in risk-free securities.

Assuming the risk-free rate of return is 12% and the average market portfolio return is 20%, the expected return from the portfolio would be:

$$(0.945 \times 20\%) + (0.055 \times 12\%) = 18.9\% + 0.66\% = 19.56\%$$

The investor in the portfolio of shares should therefore expect a return of 19.56% and if diversification has completely eliminated unsystematic risk the actual return will also be 19.56%.

The alpha factor

The alpha factor in CAPM theory is another term for abnormal return, due to the specific (diversifiable) risk of an individual security. The alpha factor is variable; it may be either positive or negative at any point in time. It must be noted, however, that by diversifying, the positive and negative alpha factors of different securities will cancel each other out. This is an important point in CAPM theory, because it explains why a security with a high beta factor might have poor returns when the market is booming and average returns are high; the explanation would be a high adverse abnormal return. Such returns are usually temporary and these alpha factors will not affect the returns of an investor who has diversified fully to eliminate unsystematic risk.

13 Methods of business valuation

PURPOSES OF BUSINESS VALUATION

There are times, unfortunately, when one has to estimate the break-up value of a business — what proceeds may be obtained from the disposal of its assets in order to meet the claims of the various classes of creditors. If this is the only course of action available, then the financial manager's role is rapidly approaching its termination.

The purpose of this chapter, however, is to review the various methods of valuing a business as a going concern. In this context the value of a business means its value to its proprietors. Admittedly, the providers of debt capital will also be interested in the total asset value as an indicator of the security for their loans. But asset values, as we shall see, do not exhaust the value of the business as an operating entity, and it is this total value which concerns the proprietors — it is their business.

When we have established this total value we can then apportion it among the individual owners, normally in relation to the amount of capital each has contributed, which in the case of a company limited by shares will be represented by their various shareholdings.

The main reason for valuing a business is as a basis for agreeing a price at which the whole or part of a proprietor's interest may be transferred to someone else. There are three common aspects of such transactions.

(a) The transfer of shares in unquoted companies: the right to transfer shares is often restricted by the articles of association, commonly at the absolute discretion of the directors. Linked with this provision there may be regulations governing how a 'fair value' for such transfer shall be established. In the case of listed companies shares will of course be bought and sold at the current market price and (except in very special circumstances) no other valuation will be needed.

(b) Taxation of capital transfers, on death or otherwise: again in the case of the listed company the market price of shares would normally be used.

(c) The amalgamation of businesses, or the takeover of one business by another: here a large-scale transfer of ownership occurs, so that even for the quoted company the market price of shares ceases to be a valid basis for the transaction. A special valuation will be needed.

METHODS OF VALUATION

In the case of an amalgamation or takeover the companies involved are undertaking a very large scale capital investment or disinvestment, and one would expect the method of evaluation to be of the same nature as those discussed in Chapter 8 — in other words, to be based on the present value of future cash flows. We will look at this possibility later in this chapter, but it is a matter of fact that DCF techniques have not been widely used for business valuation, even for mergers and acquisitions. For small share transfer and taxation purposes the work involved in cash flow analysis would rarely be justified.

The methods in common use are based on either:

(a)   asset values; or
(b)   earnings; or
(c)   some combination of these two;

and these will first be described.

It must be emphasised that any method will rely on estimates that will be subject to uncertainty. If alternative methods are applied to the same company it is likely that they will give rise to different valuations. For these two reasons it is never possible to arrive at a valuation which is uniquely 'correct'. The purpose of making valuations is to provide a framework within which it may be possible to agree an acceptable solution to the problem in hand — whether it be the establishment of a share transfer price or an amount of tax payable, or the negotiation of terms for the combination of two businesses. In the examples that follow we shall never be fixing a price — we shall be suggesting a range of possible values or a starting point for further discussion.

VALUATIONS BASED ON ASSET VALUES

There might be some occasions when the book value of the assets would be acceptable. In most cases, however, and particularly if the business were being valued for the purpose of sale, it would be necessary to revalue the assets on a more appropriate basis. This is likely to be the value of the assets to the business as a going concern.

The value to the business of freehold land and buildings would be their open market value for their existing use, and this should be established by a professional valuer. Such a valuation would automatically take account of any deterioration in the condition of the buildings.

In the case of leasehold property, the unexpired portion of the lease would also have an open market value. It is conceivable that the open market value would be excessive in relation to the discounted future earning power of the business, in which case an earnings-based valuation for the business as a whole would be more appropriate than an asset valuation. Alternatively, if a prospective buyer had the intention of altering the nature of the business, one might substitute an open-market valuation of the land and buildings based on that alternative use.

If the intention was to dispose of the land and buildings, then they should be valued at the net amount they would realise if sold.

It can be seen that the above valuation methods are similar to current cost accounting methods.

In the case of stocks and work in progress the relevant valuation would be their historical cost, although if the business were being valued for sale then it would be reasonable to substitute some approximation to their replacement value. From this starting point it would be necessary to make deductions for damaged or defective stocks, and for any stocks which are not readily saleable or which could be sold only at prices below the basic valuation.

Provisions for debts unlikely to be collected would presumably have been made in the accounts of the business, but their adequacy would need to be reviewed.

Any figure of goodwill in the company's balance sheet would be ignored, since goodwill emerges from a valuation based on earnings, and has no part in the valuation of assets.

The asset value method of valuation might be the most suitable for a property company but even in this exceptional case it is unlikely that it would be used as the only method. Applied to the calculations of a saleable value of a business it implies that the purchaser is just buying a collection of assets without regard to their earning power.

VALUATIONS BASED ON EARNINGS

A very popular method of assessing the value of a company is to use some predetermined rate of return that an investor would expect on this particular type of investment. This is customarily the simple rate of return on capital employed, such as is used in the ratio analysis of accounts. The rate is applied to the earnings of the company to arrive at the capital sum which would yield those earnings at that rate.

The earnings figure required is that which will be maintainable in future years. The valuation would be highly misleading if it were based on past experience, and immediately afterwards there was an acceleration or a falling-off in the rate of earnings. You will read sometimes about takeover offers which have proved excessive because after the acquisition the earnings of the acquired company failed to reach the forecast figure.

This can happen in spite of independent investigation by accountants, because it is of the nature of forecasts to be unreliable. However, every effort must be made to make a reliable forecast of future earnings as the basis of valuation. In most cases the forecast will be to some extent an extrapolation from past experience, and in those cases where a takeover aggressor has to make a valuation without help from the target company he will be almost entirely reliant on the past history of earnings.

If earnings have not been consistent in the past, this may be because this is the type of business which naturally has fluctuating profits (some types of jobbing and contracting work are of this nature), or is affected by a recognisable cycle of business activity. We should then take an average figure of profit over a suitable number of years as our starting point. If the profits had been showing a steady increase or decrease, then we might calculate a weighted average over perhaps three or five years, giving the heaviest weighting to the most recent results.

In every case it is important to adjust the reported profits for individual items which relate purely to past exceptional circumstances (such as abnormal remuneration to the founders of a private company) or which are dealt with differently by other companies from which the proposed capitalisation factor is being derived. The ownership or leasing of assets would fall into this category.

Instead of using a bookkeeper's rate of return it is sometimes possible to use a price/earnings ratio. A listed company will have its own P/E ratio, and one only has to decide whether the same ratio will continue to apply under future business conditions. The chances are that it will unless there is an unforeseen major change either in the economic environment or in the management of the business. The ratio may be high in relation to current earnings because investors believe that earnings will increase — and vice versa. Using a P/E ratio therefore means that you can jump directly from today's earnings to a valuation which takes account of a consensus of opinion on what future earnings will be.

If we are dealing with an unquoted company, then we should look for a quoted company (or preferably a group of quoted companies) in the same field of business and apply its P/E ratio, or a representative ratio, to the private company's results — but not without adjustment. Experience shows that the P/E ratio to be applied to a private company's results should be about half the ratio which exists for a comparable public company. If, for example, the P/E ratio of a quoted company was 12:1, then in valuing a similar private company a ratio of about 6:1 would be used.

Example 1   This example illustrates the use of an average figure earnings and also the application of a P/E ratio. The following is the balance sheet of Loafers Ltd, a private company engaged in wholesale bakery:

Loafers Ltd: balance sheet at 31 December 19X6

	£		£
1,600,000 ordinary		Goodwill	100,000
shares of 25p		Fixed assets	445,000
each	400,000	Current assets	955,000
Capital reserve	75,000		
Revenue reserve	225,000		
	700,000		
250,000 7% (formerly			
10% gross) preference			
shares of £1 each			
(redeemable in 20			
years)	250,000		
	950,000		
Current liabilities	550,000		
	1,500,000		1,500,000

The P/E ratio for public companies in the industry is approximately 15 and for a private company like Loafers Ltd the P/E ratio would therefore be about 7.5.

Mr Cakebread, the chairman and managing director, has received a bid of 35p each for the ordinary shares, and seeks advice as to whether this is a reasonable price to recommend his shareholders to accept.

The following information is relevant:

(a) Included in fixed assets are premises valued at £300,000 in January 19X0. A fair rental for the premises would be £40,000 a year at 19X6 rates which, on an estimated yield of 10% would make them now worth £400,000.

(b) On a review of the current assets it now seems desirable to make further provisions for doubtful debts £15,000 and obsolete stocks £17,000.

(c) Profits/(losses) before taxation have been:

	£
19X3	120,000
19X4	(10,000)
19X5	100,000
19X6	150,000

The forecast profit before taxation for 19X7 is £180,000.

(d)   The purchaser would redeem the preference shares at par.

Assets basis	£	£
Fixed assets	445,000	
Add: Probable appreciation of property to give current yield of 10%	100,000	
		545,000
Current assets £(955,000 − 17,000 − 15,000)	923,000	
Less: Current liabilities	550,000	
		373,000
		918,000
Deduct: Preference shareholders' entitlement		250,000
Net assets value		668,000

Net assets value per ordinary share £668,000/1,600,000= 41.75p

Without revaluing the property the net assets value per ordinary share would be £568,000/1,600,000 = 35.5p.

Earnings basis Profits/(losses)	3-year weighted average £000		3 years average £000	5 years average £000
19X3				120
19X4				(10)
19X5	100 × 1	100	100	100
19X6	150 × 2	300	150	150
19X7	180 × 3	540	180	180
	6	940	430	540
Average per annum		156.7	143.3	108.0
Taxation at say 50%		78.3	71.7	54.0
		78.4	71.6	54.0
Preference dividend		17.5	17.5	17.5
Net earnings		60.9	54.1	36.5
Capitalised at P/E ratio 7.5		£456,750	£405,750	£273,750
Value per share (1,600,000 shares)		28.5p	25.3p	17.1p
P/E ratio at bid price 35p approx (£560,000/£60,900 etc)		9.2	10.4	15.3

One is not aware of the reason for the loss incurred by the business in 19X4, nor why the 19X5 profit was below what appears otherwise to be a steady upward trend. The 19X7 forecast profit of £180,000 has not yet been achieved, of course, and without it one might not assume any trend, but rather a series of random results. If the forecast is achieved, does this suggest even higher profits in later years without any need to introduce more outside capital?

Assuming that £180,000 is a realistic figure of maintainable future profits, then the earnings valuation would be:

	£000	£000
Maintainable annual profit		180
Less: Taxation 50%	90	
Preference dividend	17.5	107.5
Net earnings		72.5
Capitalised at P/E 7.5		£543,750
Value per share		34.0p

One would have thought that a P/E ratio of 7.5 on a forecast of profit never before attained was not commercially realistic in the baking industry. If it is accepted, however, that £180,000 profit is a realistic forecast, it is worth considering how the buyer proposes redeeming the preference shares. If he were able to do this by an issue of loan stock at 12½% the above calculation could be revised as follows:

	£000
Maintainable annual profit	180
Less: Loan interest £250,000 @ 12½%	31.25
	148.75
Taxation (50%)	74.375
Net earnings	74.375
Capitalised at P/E 7.5	557.8
Value per share	34.9p (which is approximately the amount of the offer)

To summarise, the bid of 35p appears generous in relation to earnings so far achieved, but may be no more than adequate if there is a real prospect of the 19X7 forecast being achieved and maintained. In either case the bid is far below what one would believe to be a realistic value of the assets, and in fact corresponds closely with the existing book value. It is possible that by making what appears to be a fair offer in relation to profits, the bidder is hoping to gain possession of valuable assets which he might plan to sell, and to take the business into his own existing facilities.

The bid should not be accepted, and efforts should be made during the course of further negotiations to discover the real objectives of the bidder.

The above example was worked out in some detail not merely to give an illustration of particular methods of calculation but also:

(a) to show the difficulty of trying to arrive at a valuation based on past earnings;

(b) to re-emphasise that there is no such thing as an exact value for a business. There will always be a range of possible values, and which of these will be nearest to a final agreed value will depend among other things on the purpose for which the valuation is being made.

A point worth making at this stage about the earnings basis of valuation when the purpose is the sale of a business, is that the existing profits may be attributable to some extent to the efforts of the management team. If this team does not stay with the business after its change of ownership there may be difficulties, at least in the short-term, in running the business and in achieving the profits which had been forecast.

It will have been noticed that Loafers Ltd in the above example had incurred a loss in one of the years under review. Although in this case the loss had been more than compensated by later profits, it will often happen that a business which is subject to a bid will have unrelieved tax losses at the date of transfer. If the purchaser will be able to offset these losses against future profits and so reduce the future tax bill, then they have a saleable value related to that future tax relief, and this must be taken into account in arriving at a valuation of the business. It will be borne in mind that such losses can only be used by the purchaser against future profits earned from the transferred business.

COMBINED METHODS OF VALUATION

Because the assets valuation and the earnings valuation of a business are likely to differ, attempts are sometimes made to combine them into a composite valuation. This is not a scientific procedure. It seems to stem from the fallacy that there must be 'a valuation' for a business, and in most cases the effect is merely to give some spurious justification for an already negotiated value.

For the sake of completeness, the two main methods are:

(a) The Berliner method:
  (i) capitalise maintainable earnings at an acceptable rate of return;
  (ii) value net tangible assets on going-concern basis;
  (iii) take an arithmetical average of the two figures.

(b) Dual capitalisation method: this method relies on the possibility of defining two acceptable rates of return — one on tangible assets of the class existing in the business under review, and one on intangible assets (this would be a higher rate because of the lack of tangible security). If this step is possible at all then the subsequent procedure can be illustrated in the following example.

Example 2 A business has tangible assets valued at £668,000. Its maintainable earnings are £72,500. The expected yield on tangible assets is 10% and on intangible assets 15%.

  (i) Tangible assets of £668,000 with an expected rate of return of 10% means that the amount of profit attributable to the tangible assets is £66,800.

  (ii) The profit attributable to intangible assets is therefore £72,500 − 66,800 = £5,700.

  (iii) The value of the intangible assets is (£5,700 × 100)/15 = £38,000.

  (iv) The total value of the business is £668,000 + £38,000 = £706,000.

SUPER-PROFIT METHOD

The super-profit method, which has some similarity to the method just described, used to be very popular and still has some adherents, probably because it starts with the simple concept of the accountant's rate of return and finishes up rather like a Dutch auction.

We will again take an example to illustrate the steps in this method.

Example 3 The following information relates to a firm of builders' merchants:

Value of net tangible assets, say	£145,000
Normal rate of return from an investment of this type	20%
Maintainable earnings estimated at	£29,500

The method is as follows:

  (a) Calculate the expected annual profits, i.e., 20% × £145,000 = £29,000.

  (b) Calculate the super-profits, i.e., the difference between the profits at the required rate of return and the profits as actually forecast: £29,500 − £29,000 = £500 per annum.

  (c) Decide how many years' super-profits shall be included in the purchase price — say three years — and thus the 'value' of the super-profits, i.e., 3 × £500 = £1,500.

(d) Add the value of the super-profits to the value of the net tangible assets to arrive at the total business valuation: in this case, £145,000 + £1,500 = £146,500.

The super-profit value can be regarded in two ways:

(a) As a value of 'goodwill' — the business yields more than the rate of return that the buyer expects normally, so he is willing to pay more than the market value of the assets in order to get the extra profit.

(b) As a subdivision of the earnings valuation of the business — in this instance we could have said that the value of the business was £29,500 maintainable earnings capitalised at 20% = £147,500, but in doing that we should have implied that the above-average performance of this business was going to continue indefinitely. The super-profits method identifies how long these high profits are expected to last (i.e., three years) and to the extent that the number of years is realistic this is a better method than the straight capitalisation of earnings.

DISCOUNTED CASH FLOWS

Following on from this last consideration — the duration of benefits — it would have been possible to apply the discounted present value approach to the example above. We have here an annuity of £29,500. By equating it to an outlay of £147,500 we have implied a discount factor of 5.000. Look at your annuity tables under 20% and you will find that for 50 years the discount factor is 4.995. In fixing a value of £147,500, therefore, we are buying more than 50 years' profits, indeed we are buying £29,500 in perpetuity. In how many business situations would a buyer deliberately do this, or a seller expect it? (There are some, obviously, like leasing premises, but in this case we are looking at a firm of builders' merchants.)

Admittedly, in negotiating prices many factors will be taken into account including the relative strength of the negotiators, but it is desirable that negotiations should not start from the exaggerated valuations implicit in the use of the simple rate of return on capital employed.

Suppose in this instance we had started with the assumption that the earnings of £29,500 would continue for 10 years. At 20% our 10-year annuity discount factor is 4.1925, and this would have given a value to the business of £29,500 × 4.1925 = £123,680 approximately, a difference of £22,820 or 16% from the valuation given by the super-profits method. This is significant.

The discounting method also enables us to deal with:

(a) non-constant earnings, since each year's forecast earnings can be evaluated at its own discount factor;

(b) outlays connected with company acquisition — not only the initial legal and other costs, redundancy payments, and new recruitment and training costs, but also any additional finance required after the original purchase;

(c) realisation of surplus assets;

(d) the effect of the amalgamation on the cash flows of the bidding company.

What is needed is a comparison of combined cash flows over the years ahead — first of the two businesses as at present constituted and then of the new combined business. This differential cash flow should be discounted at the cost of capital (however defined) of the bidding company.

Discounting methods have not so far been widely used, because of:

(a) the complexity of the data to be handled, and its sheer volume;

(b) the difficulty of forecasting reliably;

(c) lack of clarity about the appropriate cost-of-capital rate.

The third point is the most difficult. The other difficulties are rapidly disappearing with the ready availability of computer models and the development of risk analysis techniques. In time the simplistic approach to cash flow analysis that we have today will in turn be replaced by more dynamic models.

PAYING THE ACQUISITION PRICE

Share for share deals

When the price at which a business is to be acquired has been finally settled, a further decision is required as to how it shall be paid. The main alternatives are:

(a) in shares of the acquiring company;

(b) in cash;

(c) in fixed interest securities;

(d) in convertible securities;

(e) by a combination of these methods.

Where payment by the issue of shares is decided on, then the number of shares required will be calculated from the purchase price divided by the market price (or other agreed price) per share of the acquiring company's shares.

For example, if A Ltd were buying B Ltd for £240,000 and the market price of A Ltd shares was 80p, then the number of shares to be issued in satisfaction of the purchase price would be: £240,000/£0.80 = 300,000 shares.

If the business being acquired is a company with share capital, then its shareholders will exchange their existing shares for shares issued by the acquirer. In the above example, if B Ltd had 400,000 shares in issue the shareholders would relinquish their 400,000 shares in exchange for 300,000 new A Ltd shares. The offer would be expressed as three new shares for every four now held.

How are the interests of the existing shareholders in the aggressor company affected by the creation of these new shares? It is important that the earnings obtained through the acquisition should be sufficient in relation to the new shares issued to ensure that there is no fall in the average earnings per share, i.e., no 'dilution' of the earnings per share of the aggressor company's shareholders.

If dilution does occur the share price is likely to fall. Dividends may be reduced, and the old shareholders will not have gained but suffered in consequence of the acquisition.

Example 4 Let us suppose that Alpha Ltd is to acquire 100% of the ordinary share capital of Beta Ltd by issuing its own shares. Alpha Ltd's authorised share capital is 4 million shares of 25p each, of which 3 million are already in issue. Its profit and loss account for the year to 31 December 19X0 showed:

	£
Profit before tax	240,000
Corporation tax at 50%	120,000
Earnings	120,000

EPS = £120,000/3,000,000 = 4p.

If the stock market price of the share is 40p, the value of the company on a P/E ratio is 10.

Beta Ltd has 1 million shares of 10p each in issue. Its profit and loss account for the year ended 31 December 19X0 showed:

	£
Profit before tax	60,000
Corporation tax at 50%	30,000
Earnings	30,000

EPS = £30,000/1,000,000 = 3p.

If the stock market price is 24p, the P/E ratio of Beta Ltd is 8.

With the market price per share of Alpha Ltd and Beta Ltd standing at 40p and 24p respectively, on acquisition Beta Ltd's shareholders would receive $(1,000,000 \times 24)/40 = 600,000$ shares in Alpha Ltd.

Assuming that profits would be sustained after the acquisition: EPS = £150,000/3,600,000 = 4.2p.

As the result of the acquisition, Alpha Ltd has increased its equity capital by 20% and its earnings by 25%.

What has happened to the old shareholders in Beta Ltd? They used to be entitled to earnings of £30,000 on 1,000,000 shares, i.e., 3p per share. They now hold quoted shares which they can realise, probably for more than they could have obtained for their old unquoted shares, and which in view of the increase in earnings per share of Alpha Ltd may well increase in price.

For Beta Ltd shareholders there has been a trade-off between loss of earnings (but again with hopes of increase due to the combined strengths of the new group) and other benefits.

What could be done if Beta Ltd wanted a better deal? Alpha Ltd's EPS has increased because it acquired with its own shares another company (probably a non-listed company) on a lower multiple of earnings than that applicable to its own shares. If, on the other hand, Beta Ltd had been bought out on a P/E ratio of 12 (giving that company a value of £360,000 (i.e., £30,000 × 12)), then Alpha Ltd's earnings would be diluted:

No. of shares in issue = 3,000,000 + 900,000 (£360,000/40p)
                       = 3,900,000
Earnings = £120,000 + £30,000 = £150,000
EPS = £150,000/3,900,000 = 3.8p per share

Alpha Ltd's EPS has been reduced because, in order to acquire Beta Ltd, it has increased its equity capital by 30% while increasing its earnings by only 25%. This is due to the fact that Beta Ltd has been valued on a higher multiple of earnings than Alpha Ltd.

In order to avoid the dilution of the earnings of the present members of Alpha Ltd, some other method must be devised to acquire Beta Ltd on a higher multiple of earnings. Possible alternatives would be to offer the present shareholders of Beta Ltd a mixture of cash, loan stock, convertible loan stock and shares. Let us see how these alternatives work if Beta Ltd is valued on a multiple of 12 at £360,000.

Cash or loan stock

Alpha Ltd raises £360,000 in cash at an interest rate of 12%, or it issues at par £360,000 of 12% loan stock. Alpha Ltd is therefore issuing no additional equity but has to pay £43,200 (12% of £360,000) interest every year, such interest being allowed as a charge for corporation tax purposes. A proforma consolidated profit and loss account based on this proposal would show:

	£
Profit before tax and interest	300,000
Less: Interest	43,200
	256,800
Corporation tax at 50%	128,400
Earnings	128,400

EPS = £128,400/3,000,000 = 4.3p compared to the existing 4.0p

Loan stock and shares

Alpha Ltd issues at par £180,000 of £12% loan stock and £180,000 worth of shares which will involve the issue of 450,000 shares valued at 40p each. A proforma consolidated profit and loss account based on this proposal would show:

	£
Profit before tax and interest	300,000
Less: Interest (12% of £180,000)	21,600
	278,400
Corporation tax at 50%	139,200
Earnings	139,200

EPS = £139,200/3,450,000 = 4.03p compared to the existing 4.0p

Beta Ltd's shareholders now get a high price for their shares and an improvement in their earnings (interest £43,200 subject to personal tax instead of potential maximum dividends of £30,000 subject to personal tax), but they have surrendered their voting power and any possibility of future earnings or share price growth.

Convertible loan stock

The advantage of receiving convertible loan stock from the viewpoint of the shareholders of Beta Ltd is that the stock should provide them with a better income than before while at the same time providing them with potential capital growth if conversion into equity takes place.

As far as Alpha Ltd is concerned, the interest payable on the stock should not dilute the earnings of the company in the initial years, and if (as is hoped) the earnings of the company, together with the savings of interest, have increased by the time the stock is converted into equity, the additional equity can be absorbed without reducing EPS.

As a rule of thumb, convertible loan stock should be convertible over a two-year period (commencing three years after the date of issue) at a premium of 10–20% above the existing share price. With that in mind, let us examine the effect of Alpha Ltd's issuing £360,000 of 10% convertible loan stock which can be converted in three years' time into equity on the basis of 20 shares for every £9 of stock. A proforma consolidated profit and loss account based on this proposal would show:

	£
Profit before tax and interest	300,000
Less: Interest (10% × £360,000)	36,000
	264,000
Corporation tax at 50%	132,000
Earnings	132,000

Basic EPS = £132,000/3,000,000 = 4.4p compared to the existing 4.0p

On the assumption that all the loan stock is in due course converted into equity — in which case 800,000 additional shares (£360,000/9 × 20) will be issued — the fully diluted EPS will be: £150,000/3,800,000 = 3.95p.

However, it is to be hoped that in three years' time the group's earnings will have increased to a figure well in excess of £150,000, so that there should be no dilution in earnings.

WHEN EARNINGS DILUTION IS ACCEPTABLE

It might be concluded from what has been said above that dilution of earnings must be avoided at all cost. However, there are two cases where a dilution of earnings might be accepted on an acquisition if there were other advantages to be gained.

The first of these cases involves a trading company with high earnings, but with few assets, which may want to increase its assets base by acquiring a company which is strong in assets but weak in earnings so that assets and earnings get more into line with each other. In this case, dilution in earnings is compensated for by an increase in net asset backing.

Example 5   Earnings Ltd has an issued capital of 2,000,000 £1 ordinary shares. Net assets (excluding goodwill) are £2,500,000 and earnings average around £1,500,000 per annum. The company is valued by the stock market on a P/E ratio of 8. Assets Ltd has an issued capital of 1,000,000 ordinary £1 shares. Net assets (excluding goodwill) are £3,500,000 and earnings average around £400,000 per annum. The shareholders of Assets Ltd accept an all-equity offer from Earnings Ltd valuing each share in Assets Ltd at £4. We will consider Earnings Ltd's earnings and assets per share before and after the acquisition of Assets Ltd.

Before the acquisition of Assets Ltd:

Earnings per share (EPS) = £1,500,000/2,000,000 = 75p.
Assets per share (APS) = £2,500,000/2,000,000 = £1.25.

After the acquisition of Assets Ltd: Assets Ltd's EPS figure is 40p (£400,000/ 1,000,000) and the company is being bought out on a multiple of 10 at £4 per share. As the takeover consideration is being satisfied by shares, Earnings Ltd's earnings will be diluted because Earnings Ltd is valuing Assets Ltd on a higher multiple of earnings than itself. Earnings Ltd will have to issue 666,667 shares valued at £6 each (earnings of 75p per share at a multiple of 8) to satisfy the £4,000,000 consideration.

EPS = £1,900,000/2,666,667 = 71.25 (lower than the previous 75p)
APS = £6,000,000/2,666,667 = £2.25 (higher than the previous £1.25)

If Earnings Ltd is still valued on the stock market on a P/E of 8, the share price should recede by approximately 30p (8 × (75p − 71.25)) but because the asset backing has been increased substantially the company will probably be valued on a higher rating than 8.

The second case where a company might be willing to accept earnings dilution involves an acquisition whereby the 'quality' of the acquired company's earnings is superior to that of the acquiring company.

Listed companies in different industries are given different ratings. A retail departmental store like Marks and Spencer is valued on a higher P/E ratio than an industrial company like ICI. The reason for the former company's higher rating is that its profits are stable and consistent (because it is selling necessities like food and clothing) whereas the profits of the latter company depend very much on the economic climate and fluctuate in accordance with it. The 'quality' of earnings is therefore of paramount importance when determining the rating of a company.

As another example, brewery companies are valued on higher multiples than tobacco companies. If, therefore, a tobacco company acquires a brewery company, dilution of earnings will take place as it did when Imperial Tobacco took over Courage Breweries. However, the share prices should not suffer as a result of the takeover because the overall quality of earnings should compensate for the dilution of earnings.

14   Mergers and acquisitions

REASONS FOR MERGERS

There are a number of reasons why a company may seek a merger:

(a) A frequent reason for an agreed takeover is that a large company or group decides to enter a new market, possibly in another country, as its researches indicate growth potential.

(b) Management acquisition often fuels plans for a merger or acquisition. If a company has inadequate management to sustain desired growth rates then it may seek to merge or acquire a company whose management is more competent and aggressive. Also, the ownership of private companies often parallels management and, therefore mergers may be arranged to provide management succession. With quoted companies, external management succession is sometimes provided by agreed merger, but probably more frequently by an uninvited offer.

(c) Growth may often be obtained more cheaply and faster by acquisition.

(d) Financial motivations.

FINANCIAL ASPECTS

There may be many varied considerations and motives behind a merger, amongst which financial motives are often foremost. Alongside these financial motives we may also note certain financial prerequisites for a merger.

One, not unusual, financial motive for an acquisition can arise when the stock market is underestimating the real value of a company. If a company's stock market price is low in relation to its potential, it is an ideal victim for a takeover bid.

Another common motive for a merger or acquisition lies in the area of taxation and tax benefits. There can be little doubt that the high level of taxation has been a factor stimulating merger activity in the post-war period. For example, an important reason for the purchase of the Cunard Steam Ship Company by Trafalgar House Investments was the tax benefits accruing from Cunard's accumulated tax losses of £6 million. Indeed, tax considerations can be regarded as a key motive in mergers. Generally the tax benefit stems from the fact that one of the firms has a tax loss carry-forward, which can be applied against future income for up to seven years. Two situations could actually exist. A company with a tax loss carry-forward could acquire a profitable company in order to utilise the tax loss carry-forward. In this case the acquiring firm would boost the combination's earnings by reducing the taxable income of the acquired firm. If the profitable firm had not been acquired, the tax loss carry-forward might not have been used. The benefits of a profitable firm acquiring a firm having such a tax loss carry-forward are equally obvious.

A third 'financial motive' for merger is that of increasing liquidity. The combination of a small and large firm, or two small firms, into a larger corporation may provide the owners of the small firm with greater liquidity. This is because of the higher marketability associated with the shares of larger firms.

Lastly, a highly desirable motive or perhaps a prerequisite for merger is 'synergy'. 'Synergy' is where the combined earnings of two companies as a merged company exceed the sum of the earnings as separate companies. The prospect of synergy resulting from economies in, for example, production and distribution can add value to the merged company.

FINANCIAL EVALUATION

It is an axiom that a merger must be financially sound. A major task of the acquiring company in the merger process is therefore that of carrying out a thorough financial evaluation of the target company and how a merger might affect all aspects of its financial position. There are a number of bases for such a financial evaluation.

A key basis for evaluation is *earnings per share;* for if the bid for a company is to succeed, the offeror must bid more than the current market value of the company's shares and, if the takeover is to have any financial advantage to the offeror company, it must be in a position to increase the level of earnings that the offeree company could attain on its own. Since, in theory, the current market value of the offeree's shares will reflect future earnings and dividends, the offeror company must base its valuation of the company on expected future earnings. Earnings per share are reflected in price/earnings ratios and are important in determining the values that will be established in a merger. The analysis begins with historical data on the firm's earnings, whose past growth rates, future trends, and variability are important determinants of the earnings multiplier, or P/E ratio, that will prevail after the merger.

The earnings per share are likely to change as a result of a merger. Generally the resulting earnings per share differ from the pre-merger earnings per share for both the acquiring and the acquired firm. They depend largely on the ratio of exchange and pre-merger earnings of each firm. Finally, it can be noted that the financial manager will often be looking for a reduction in variability of earnings per share or some type of long-run increase in per share earnings that will increase the market value of the firm's shares.

A second key financial variable and consequently an important basis for evaluation is the *market price per share*. This has a strong influence in merger terms as the financial manager seeks to maximise the market price per share in negotiating a merger. He will also pay considerable attention to market price per share because only if the market price of shares in the combined enterprise increases over the long run, will the firm's overall objective of maximisation of owners' wealth be achieved.

The key relationship affecting the merged firm's earnings per share and market price per share is the relationship between the price/earnings ratio of the acquired firm and that of the acquiring firm.

Although earnings per share and market price per share are the key bases of a financial evaluation a number of other aspects may influence merger terms and therefore need to receive some attention in a financial valuation.

The *operating and financial risk* resulting from a merger must be considered in any financial evaluation of a merger candidate. Generally, operating risk, which reflects the stability of sales, is considered in making the initial merger inquiry. The financial risk, which depends on the firm's financial structure, must normally be evaluated through a study of post-merger financial structure. Occasionally, a desire to change the firm's financial risk is the primary motive for a merger. An accurate estimation of the changes in risk is important because of its effect on the post-merger valuation of the firm's shares. If the combined operating and financial risk increases as a result of a merger, investors will discount the firm's earnings at a higher rate, thereby lowering its market price. The decreased market price will be reflected in a lower P/E ratio. If the combined risk decreases, an increase in the market price of the firm's shares and its P/E ratio can be expected. An awareness of these effects is important in forecasting the post-merger price per share. Failure to recognise these effects could result in an incorrect merger decision.

The effects of a proposed merger on the *financial leverage* or structure of the resulting enterprise is also of considerable importance in the valuation process. If the firm increases its leverage as the result of a merger, its expected earnings and dividends will be discounted by investors at a higher rate. The net effect will be to lower the value of the owners' holdings if earnings are not expected to increase sufficiently to offset the increased financial risk associated with the firm.

Net current assets per share are also likely to have an influence on merger terms because they represent the amount of liquidity that may be obtained from a company in a merger.

Of minor relevance in the financial valuation process are dividends per share and book value. Dividends per share do not normally enter into the merger decision since the primary concern of the acquiring firm is earnings per share and these are a prerequisite to the payment of dividends. Nevertheless, a financial manager must still look to ensure that the merger dividend is at least the same as the pre-merger dividend in order to stabilise the market price of the firm's shares.

Book value per share is also usually irrelevant in merger negotiations. Yet if book values substantially exceed market values, they may well have an impact on merger terms. Also, if the firm being acquired is being obtained only for its assets, then the book value per share may be helpful in determining the purchase price per share.

METHODS OF PAYMENT

The final financial aspects of a merger which we need to consider are the proposed methods of payment.

Cash

If the bidder has cash available, cash will be the cheapest consideration in the long-term, as the acceptor of cash would have no future shares in the equity of the bidder, which would not be 'diluted'. If the liquid resources of the bidder were restricted, however, cash would be expensive in the short term. From the offeree's viewpoint cash payment holds a major disadvantage, in that he would be subject to immediate capital gains tax and would have no further equity interest in the company. Cash does hold the advantage of allowing immediate reinvestment in shares but this must be offset against the capital gains tax liability and the relatively high dealings cost of a purchase of securities.

Ordinary shares

Payment by means of an exchange of ordinary shares is of advantage to the offeree if he gains an agreement which values his shares more highly than those of the offeror; but the offeror company will experience a dilution in equity and its share price will fall somewhat when its takeover attempt is made public. From the offeree's point of view, if his shares are valued on a lower basis than those of the offeror for example, he may still relinquish his interest in the company under a bid for a higher real value in the interest he acquires in the offeror company. The major determinant is the relative real value of the equity whilst he also incurs no immediate capital gains liability or stamp duty liability and he will maintain a continuing interest in the bidding company and therefore incur no dealing costs in the purchase of securities.

Debenture

Payment by debenture is another alternative. This would be costly to the offeror in a time of high interest rates but his equity would not be diluted. The offeree would incur no capital gains tax liability but would have a fixed interest security instead of equity.

Convertible loan stock

Finally, payment may be made in the form of convertible unsecured loan stock. The offeror would be able to offer a lower coupon than for a normal loan stock but dilution of equity could arise. The offeree, on the other hand, would incur no immediate capital gains tax. Much would depend on the conversion terms and the record shows that these have often been very much weighted in favour of the offeror.

The different means of payment available are an important financial consideration in a merger or acquisition because they carry a number of advantages/disadvantages for the merging companies. They are, consequently, the subject of much discussion, with considerable negotiating skills required of the negotiators.

THE MERGER PROCESS

A 'successful merger' can be defined as 'one which fulfils most of the expectations held by the parties at the time the deal was struck — rather than just a merger which succeeds in being consummated'.

A merger needs to be judged against strategic criteria which may be divided into three heads: business fit, management, and financial terms. The successful merger relies very much on thorough homework and we can identify a number of stages in the merger/acquisition process.

The first stage in a successful merger is that of *screening*. The 'screen' may be either a positive or negative one, the difference between which can be explained by the following examples. If a manufacturer of motor bikes is looking for a merger to increase the size of his business, widen his management resources and improve his standing with customers, his screen for business fit might be that of another motor bike manufacturer or one of his subassembly suppliers — a positive test. A negative screen might be: 'I will not merge with a business if I am ignorant of both its manufacturing processes and markets.'

Following the screening stage the prospective offeror needs to do some detailed homework on the serious candidates for merger which have resulted from the screening. This involves detailed investigation of the three principal criteria — business fit, management, and finance. The investigation should ensure realism about the strengths and weaknesses both of one's own company and the prospective merger candidate. It can also be noted that the offeror during this stage should be seeking to estimate the negotiating position of the company owners.

The next stage is that of the approach and negotiations, but before an approach is made the offeror needs to check that his own case is carefully prepared. He must consider two objectives: the benefits to be obtained and the attendant risks; and the negotiating positions to be taken — remembering that it is the distinction between the two objectives rather than their content which is most important.

The negotiation stage can be something of a 'ritual dance', as, in order to secure the highest price the seller makes noises to the effect that he is not particularly keen to sell, and the buyer similarly implies that his first offer is not far from his limit price. Two 'rules' may be identified with regard to negotiating. First, the seller needs to decide the minimum price acceptable and the buyer needs to decide the maximum he is prepared to pay. Second, one needs to distinguish reality from negotiating posture and hence one must remember that there are very few true mergers and very many acquisitions, due to inequality in 'financial muscle'. Equal mergers are also made practically impossible by the management terms, i.e., any business unit nearly always has to have someone in charge and the others have to accept instructions.

REVERSE BIDS

Usually it is a larger company which bids for a smaller one; a 'reverse bid', however, is where a smaller company bids for the larger. Such a reverse takeover may occur for a number of reasons:

(a) The smaller company is listed but the larger company is not and therefore in order to keep the listing without having to pay costs in obtaining a new one the smaller listed company makes the takeover.

(b) The law requires that pre-acquisition profits be frozen, and so if the smaller company has large undistributed profits its profits would be frozen. It may therefore make sense for it to take over the larger company.

(c) Takeover by the smaller firm would also be more appropriate if it had the better record and more promising future.

THE CITY CODE

In 1959 the Governor of the Bank of England set up a City working party for the purpose of considering good business practice in the conduct of takeovers and mergers. The deliberations of this working party resulted in the publication in 1968 of *The City Code on Takeovers and Mergers*, which is regularly revised so that as far as practicable it meets the needs of the times — the present code is dated May 1986.

The Code is administered and enforced by the Panel on Takeovers and Mergers, a body representative of those using the securities market. In 1978 this Panel came under the control of the new Council for the Securities Industry.

In the Introduction to the Code it was made clear that persons engaging in merger transactions should realise that the spirit as well as the precise wording of the principles and rules should be observed. The general principles of the Code are concerned with ensuring that all shareholders of an offeree company are treated in an equitable manner. Although the City Code does not have the force of law behind it — this is considered to be a strength rather than a weakness, partly because of the 'spirit' factor and partly because of the speed with which it can be amended — it does still have considerable powers, with available penalties ranging from private reprimand to suspension of an offender and withdrawal of the facilities of the securities markets, and in certain cases referral to the Department of Trade.

The present Code contains six sections:

(a) *Introduction* This states that the Code applies to offers for public companies both listed and unlisted, but not to offers for private companies, or non-UK companies.

(b) *Procedure*

(c) *Definitions of the Code*

(d) *General principles* In other words, the 'spirit' of the Code. This section sets the tone of the Code and applies to 'areas and circumstances' not explicitly covered by any Rule. The section includes the following principles:

(i) Shareholders should be given sufficient information to form a judgement on a bid.

(ii) Directors of a target company should act in the best interests of their shareholders.

(iii) Directors should obtain competent independent advice.

(iv) All shareholders of the same class should be treated similarly.

(v) All parties should not behave in a way which would result in a false market.

(vi) Documents addressed to shareholders should be prepared with the same care as a prospectus.

(vii) Anyone making a bid should be sure that he will in fact be able to implement it.

(e) *Rules* The City Code lays down a detailed series of rules which must be adhered to throughout the process of completing a merger or amalgamation.

(f) *Practice notes* This is the sixth section of the Code and the 'Practice notes' contained therein seek to offer guidance on the detailed operation of the principles and rules. The full Panel meets quarterly to receive a report from its Director-General and to discuss policy. The panel may also meet to consider: a particular case brought before it by the Director-General; a ruling by the Director-General which has been contested by the parties to the bid;

disciplinary action on an alleged breach of the Code; new legislative or other proposals affecting the panel's area of operations.

THE MONOPOLIES AND MERGERS COMMISSION

In 1948 the Monopolies and Restrictive Practices Commission was set up with the power to investigate and report monopoly situations referred to it by the then Board of Trade. A monopoly was stated to exist when one company produced at least one-third of the supply of particular goods. The 1965 Monopolies and Mergers Act widened the powers of the Commission so that the Board of Trade were now able to refer to it prospective or actual mergers, provided either that the resulting company would have a monopoly or that the assets acquired were worth £5 million or more. Not only could a merger be held up until the Monopolies Commission had reported, but if it were found that a monopoly was against the public interest then various remedies could be implemented, including the forced division of an existing company. The Commission became the Monopolies and Mergers Commission under the Fair Trading Act 1973.

The influence of the Monopolies Commission extends beyond the limited number of investigations in which it has been involved. It is argued that many potential merger situations have not gone ahead because they exhibited characteristics similar to one or other of the referred mergers. In addition, many merger proposals now contain a clause stating that if the proposal should be referred to the Monopolies Commission, then the proposal would lapse.

ROLE OF MERCHANT BANKS

It is almost inconceivable that a company should involve itself in any merger or acquisition deal without seeking the aid of financial advisers. The financial advice almost inevitably will come from a merchant bank; the reason for this is essentially twofold. First, although statute law gives a merchant bank no right to advise on mergers or takeovers, an offeror will need to circulate the offer to the shareholders of the target company and The Prevention of Fraud (Investments) Act 1958 restricts those who may issue such circulars to, for example, members of a recognised stock exchange, licensed dealers and exempted dealers — merchant banks being one of the latter. Second, *The City Code on Takeovers and Mergers* obliges companies to seek independent advice, and, in practice, because merchant banks have established over a number of years 'corporate finance departments' which specialise in the sponsorship of capital issues as they relate to mergers and acquisitions, they are employed as the independent financial advisers.

The role of a merchant bank in a merger or takeover bid involves a number of activities. Continual research must be performed by the merchant bank and the acquisitive company; the ideas and proposals emerging from this will then be subject to in-depth study by the bank involving the collection of both commercial and financial data. The merchant bank will then need to consider the strategy with which the emerging possibilities should be pursued. Once this has been considered the all-important approach is made. Here the merchant bank can often be actively involved, as the approach may be made by the merchant bank of the acquisitive company to the target company's merchant bank. The merchant bank and its client will act in tandem, negotiating terms likely to carry the support of the board and shareholders of the offeree company whilst still being demonstrably favourable to the offeror and carrying the support of its shareholders. Then, where a bid proceeds, the merchant bank acts as the coordinator of the implementation stage, including preparing an offer document containing profit forecasts and working capital statements.

The involvement of a merchant bank in the merger 'business' is not restricted to quoted companies; where the subject of the transaction is a private company the merchant bank may still be deeply involved — assisting in evaluating a possible purchase, working out strategy, handling negotiations and coordinating the steps necessary for a concluded transaction.

The role of merchant banks in international mergers and acquisitions must be noted. A number of leading merchant banks have established corporate finance departments in overseas market places. Generally speaking, advice is needed in the country of residence of the target company; for example, a UK company bidding in the US would probably need to have the local advice of acquisitions and mergers experts on Wall Street. These overseas corporate finance departments therefore serve to advise on cross-frontier takeovers and mergers. The merchant bank plays a leading role in the business of mergers, etc.; many of these banks have long-term relationships with companies as their financial advisers, but although in the past such relationships may have been initiated merely on introduction from a mutual friend, the modern merchant banker must present his skills and expertise to a prospective client before securing any mandate.

RECENT MERGER ACTIVITY

The recent 'merger mania' in the City provides us with plentiful material for studying the practice of merger deals. During the first quarter of 1986 the value of corporate takeover bids launched in the UK has amounted to £20 billion; this compares with £3.2 billion for the first quarter of 1985 and £6.4 billion for the whole of 1985.

This frenetic activity is perhaps partly explained by a possible correlation between the activity on the takeover front and generally rising equity values on the stock market. Yet it seems that the main cause lies in a change in the rules governing mergers and acquisitions. It is true to say that the bidder has always had some advantage over the offeree; he is able to plan any merger for months before announcing a bid, whilst under *The City Code on Takeovers and Mergers* the offeree board may have little more than three weeks to mount a defence. Even so, until the recent battles developed for control of Imperial Group and Distillers, the Office of Fair Trading offered a haven for target companies, who could look to a Monopolies Commission referral on various grounds — the strongest being the potential creation of a monopoly situation. The rules have now been changed; Sir Gordon Borrie, Director-General of OFT has waved in a new era, singularly beneficial to the bidder by way of permitting a corporate bidder to refine its takeover proposals should they warrant referral.

It is evident that Sir Gordon Borrie's acceptance of refinement has widespread implications: it is clear now that any bid with an attractive premium will almost certainly succeed (in the absence of competition) and that the target company has little defence. Many industrialists, however, view the new 'refinement' policy of the government as the instigator of chaos in merger policy and procedures and consequently it is now under review.

Index